My View, My Voice

21 STRATEGIES for POWERFUL, PERSUASIVE WRITING

Rebekah Coleman and Carolyn Greenberg

Foreword by Pam Allyn

Publishing Credits

Corinne Burton, M.A.Ed., *Publisher*
Conni Medina, M.A.Ed., *Managing Editor*
Nika Fabienke, Ed.D., *Content Director*
Veronique Bos, *Creative Director*
Shaun N. Bernadou, *Art Director*
Noelle Cristea, M.A.Ed., *Editor*
Regina Frank, *Graphic Designer*

Image Credits

p.7, p. 31, p.39 Public Domain; p.23 Courtesy Simon Davis/DFID; p.109 Library of Congress [LC-DIG-ppmsca-38698]; p.157, p.160 Courtesy LitLife, Inc.; all other images from iStock and/or Shutterstock.

Standards

Shell Education
A division of Teacher Created Materials
5301 Oceanus Drive
Huntington Beach, CA 92649-1030
www.tcmpub.com/shell-education
ISBN 978-1-4258-1698-8

Table of Contents

Acknowledgments

Thank you to the wise and wonderful team with whom we work at LitLife each day—passionate educators who nurture and guide students and teachers to find joy, hope, and a deep love of learning in classrooms around the world. It is a gift to be part of this community. We would particularly like to acknowledge and thank Pam and Jim Allyn, who compassionately and powerfully use their voices to advocate for children each and every day. Thank you, Pam and Jim, for inspiring us to write this book and for all you have done to help make it happen. We would also like to thank the great team at Teacher Created Materials for giving us this wonderful opportunity.

Rebekah: I would like to thank my beloved family and friends, you know who you are, who loved, laughed, and journeyed alongside me and gave me the courage to find my voice. And thank you to the teachers and librarians in my life who believe deeply that humanity is stronger when we use our voices and express our views with confidence and courage. I would particularly like to thank my family, especially my mom and dad, who lead by example and set the bar so high, and Sarah, Nick, Cole, and Attie, who have been there each step of the way. And to my beloved Hannah, Kate, Erin, and Ian—thank you for your love, support, and inspiration.

Carolyn: Although my parents sometimes told me as a child that "children should be seen and not heard" (probably when they simply needed some peace and quiet to relax from their busy days), I am both certain and glad that they did not really believe that. They always taught me to ask questions, listen to others, and express myself and my views, and I thank them for that. I also would like to thank my entire family and many friends who have always supported my passions, projects and dreams. Your encouragement and love mean the world to me. John, Melanie, and Abby, my wonderful husband and children, I truly could not do what I do without you. Thanks to Cosmo, too—my furry little work partner.

Rebekah and Carolyn dedicate this book to Hannah, Kate, Erin, Melanie, and Abby—our five smart, funny, fierce, brave, and wondrous daughters who are fearlessly discovering the power of their own voices and who inspire us, challenge us, and teach us each day. We love you and hope you will always have the courage to find your voices and use them to speak up for others, against injustices—big and small.

Foreword

This is the series we've been waiting for. In the last 10 years, educators have recognized the profound importance of the role of persuasive writing in the lives of students, for their academic and personal development, and for their success across all the content areas. This is the genre that crosses all disciplines, that goes between home and school, enters into the community, and can change the world. It is the genre that helps a student become a more engaged, confident and impactful member of every community he or she belongs to. And yet, the support for teachers and students in this area of writing instruction has been quite limited. It's been hard for educators to find examples of persuasive writing that really match students where they are at, and it's been challenging to find the kinds of dynamic lessons that really speak to the immediacy and importance of this form of writing while maintaining the spirit of joy and fun in the genre.

Until now.

A brilliant, beautiful, bold series chock-full of guidance, lessons, and concrete examples of how we can best help our students write persuasively, providing us the inspiration we've needed for how to help our students write well in the persuasive genre and also the practical pathways to really make it happen.

Our authors are two master educators: Carolyn Greenberg and Rebekah Coleman. Greenberg and Coleman have been on the ground working at every grade level, side by side with students, coaching and supporting teachers nationwide as leaders in professional development.

They are humane, deeply wise, and generous teachers of teachers and brilliant writers of lessons and strategies we can use with our students to ensure that they write powerfully and well. It is just right that these two extraordinary educators should be the pair who lead us forward with this groundbreaking work on this most urgent subject: persuasive writing.

Young people want to know: *What will make a difference in the world? They want to know: How can their voices matter?* They want to know that their ideas and stories will be heard. And in this key time in the world, their voices and ideas can and should matter, from social media to op-eds, from essays to text messages, from book reviews to blogs. Persuasive writing is no longer an optional teaching idea; it is essential to the deepest work we do in the classroom.

Yet as educators we have faced challenges in the teaching of persuasive writing—we have grappled with how to guide our students to deep understandings of the genre through discussion of evidence, opinion, facts, and argument. We have grappled with how we teach specific lessons that can really matter to our students, those who struggle as writers and those who thrive. This series answers all this for us and more. It is abundant with lessons, ideas, definitions, craft moves, and samples we can really use. It is a treasure.

Grades 3 to 5 are crucial for learning to write deeply and profoundly. Our students must go deeper into content-area reading and writing. They are becoming more and more conscious of the world around them and persuasive writing brings their voices into the world. This series is an essential

Foreword *(cont.)*

companion for all of us as educators, your seminal guide through the thicket of how to teach evidence based writing, build effective arguments, sift through facts and opinions, build validity of multiple viewpoints and ensure credibility of sources. The authors guide us through this complex terrain, making it simpler, easier to access, and most of all, fun.

Finally: voice. Greenberg and Coleman celebrate the profound power of children's voices. They center the series around the potential within all our students to have big ideas, to create them, and to find the evidence and the craft of writing to articulate them best.

This is no small thing. Greenberg and Coleman understand children in these grade levels—their growth and development, their hopes and dreams—and they know how to inspire them, engage them, and uplift them. Argument, persuasion, opinion—all of this is about fearlessness, about tackling an idea and building a case. It's not easy to teach fearlessness, but that's what Greenberg and Coleman do by setting forth the tools that can help students become just that.

This is an important series from important writers at an important time. The world is changing before our eyes and so the power of persuasion is more crucial than ever before: our students can and will use this powerful tool to connect to others, to have agency in the world, and to be the kind of citizens, family members, and school leaders who change the world. I am very pleased and honored to welcome you to this special and essential experience, a superb teaching resource to inform your teaching, deeply impact your students, and bring powerful writing into the world.

—**Pam Allyn,** *Founding Director of LitWorld*

Introduction

"Don't raise your voice. Improve your argument."
—Desmond Tutu

Why Persuasive Writing Matters

Welcome to *My View, My Voice: 21 Strategies for Powerful, Persuasive Writing*. You may be wondering, "Will this book help me as a teacher of persuasive writing?" We say, "Yes, it will!" Let us persuade you as to why.

Persuasive messages abound in today's world. Each day, we experience a constant shower of words and images meant to influence our views in hopes that we will spend money, join a cause, cast a vote, or otherwise change the course of our thoughts and actions. Students are no exception. Students are inundated with advertising via commercials, billboards, T-shirts, cereal boxes, viral Internet ads, apps, and video games. Some companies even bank on long-term brand recognition—most students do not understand what GEICO does, but they love that gecko!

We navigate this daily bombardment and *try* to make wise choices, which is not always easy. Conflicting ideas, emotional appeals, faulty logic, and fallacious evidence cloud the picture. It is challenging and time-consuming to vet sources and tease out fact from falsehood.

Thus, many of us are not thoughtfully critical consumers of the opinions and arguments that surround us. This can have negative consequences. Some people may be so easily swayed that they never form stable, actionable opinions. Others form superficial views that are based on how they "feel" rather than solid reasoning and evidence. When pressed to defend such views, the lack of sound backing may cause them to falter or skirt the issue with a defensive, "Well, that's my opinion," or "That's just how I feel." They may hold so tightly to a stance that they refuse to hear anyone else, thus making collaboration, compromise, and progress impossible. Additionally, loose understanding of the reasoning for their own convictions may render them vulnerable to being taken advantage of by people who maliciously seek to influence their behavior for personal gain.

With undoubted advances in technology and communication, the future we face will likely contain more persuasive appeals than ever before. What innovative methods will advertisers, politicians, news media outlets, and others seeking to spread their messages develop in the future? Who knows? We all may be receiving messages telepathically or via personal drones before we know it!

This means we, as teachers, must prepare students now.

Introduction *(cont.)*

We need to explicitly teach our students how to become confident, critical consumers of others' opinions and arguments. Students must practice exploring conflicting views and information on a topic and keeping an open mind to possibilities they may not yet have considered. They must learn to distinguish between an argument based on facts and logic and one that may be enticingly loud, simple, and clear, but not necessarily true. They must build strong skills and strategies to evaluate the soundness of the reasoning, relevance, and credibility of evidence with a goal of establishing personal views that are truly informed, not simply emotional. They must not only believe in their views but also be able to express them clearly and stand behind them with logic and evidence. Such skills are critical for both success in school as writers of opinions and arguments (Graff and Birkenstein 2010; Hillocks 2010) and to productively engage with others in society (Andriessen 2006).

We, as teachers, can help. Even very young students can begin to understand what opinions and reasons are. We can help them become aware that not everyone has the same view, and because of that, we can learn from each other. **Students should learn to recognize and think critically when others try to influence them in the real world. They can develop awareness of audience and appreciate the power and importance of sharing one's opinion to persuade others.** They should experience and enjoy writing in many different forms as they use words, visuals, and traditional and digital tools to express themselves.

Older students are ready to move from opinion writing to the more sophisticated subgenre of argumentation. This will compel them to explore increasingly complex, arguable issues that have broad impact on communities, countries, and the world. They understand and demonstrate that arguments can be good and productive when engaging with purpose and diplomacy. They can weigh evidence from a variety of sources to develop and support their thinking to convince readers of their opinions. They can be guided to consider what it means to be credible and to evaluate arguments of others in order to make effective choices.

Persuasive Writing: writing in which the author attempts to persuade the reader to believe or do something

Opinion Writing:

- The author shares an opinion on a topic.
- The author provides reasons to support the opinion.

Argument Writing:

- The author takes a stance on an arguable issue.
- The author provides researched reasoning and evidence.
- The author shows the audience that the author's stance is the strongest of all sides of the argument.

The *My View, My Voice* series challenges K–8 students to explore, analyze, and evaluate the views of others in order to develop and share their own views. Our goal is for students to not only *learn to argue* effectively but also to *argue to learn*—an important distinction that Jerry Andriessen describes in "Arguing to Learn" (Andriessen 2006). One refers to a student's ability to articulate his or her views and reasoning effectively. The other suggests a willingness to engage in a respectful exchange of views with others in search of new information and insight. We assert that both of these capacities are essential to be an effective persuasive writer. This book, for third-, fourth-, and fifth-grade teachers, provides age-appropriate learning opportunities and strategies to help students build the skills and strategies they need to *learn to argue* and *argue to learn.*

Learning to argue and arguing to learn suggest that students should not only develop opinions and arguments but that they should also actively engage in social discourse to express and refine their ideas. Having a view on a topic goes hand in hand with sharing it with others. Never before have there been more opportunities and tools to share opinions with friends, the local community, and even worldwide! Students today are sharing their views in a myriad of ways: social media, blogs, video game conversations, and more. In fact, 59 percent of kids join social networks before the age of 10 (Lange 2014). It is human nature for people to want to share their ideas and persuade others to agree with them. However, what is really important is not just *that kids are sharing their opinions* but *how effectively* kids are sharing their opinions. When we shout our opinions loudly or argue a point without listening to the other side, we are arguing just to be heard but not to work together to achieve a common goal (Andriessen 2006).

To be clear, this work has a larger purpose. Engagement in persuasive writing provides students with an avenue to examine a topic, develop informed views through the examination of the facts as well as the views of others, and express their voices, defending their ideas with logical reasoning based on evidence. This skill set is essential to students as it is a crucial component of being an active and responsible citizen in society. The freedom of expression is the cornerstone of the democratic process. Benjamin Franklin wrote, "Freedom of speech is a principal pillar of a free government: When this support is taken away, the constitution of a free society is dissolved."

We want students of all ages to understand that they have views and voices that empower them to engage in productive debate and make positive changes in both small and big ways. This is particularly important for students who come from vulnerable communities and marginalized groups. Finding one's voice and learning to use it effectively can change the trajectory of a life for the better (Carnegie Council on Advancing Adolescent Literacy 2010).

In recent years, curricular reforms in schools have recognized and elevated the importance of argumentative reading and writing skills. This is particularly evident in the Common Core Standards for English language arts for grades 6–12 (National Governors Association, Council of Chief State School Officers 2010). Despite the strong focus on persuasive writing in today's educational standards and testing, teaching persuasive writing remains challenging for many educators. As teachers and leaders in the educational field, we have worked with a multitude of teachers and schools from around the country. We have discovered that the art of persuasive writing is not well understood, well taught, or even enjoyed by many teachers. Likewise, and perhaps as a result, many students struggle with persuasive writing. Research confirms this observation (Newell et al. 2011, 276–277). We provide five of the most common challenges and explain how this text addresses them.

Five Key Obstacles to Successful Teaching of Persuasive Writing

1. Persuasive writing is hard!

Explanation: Effective persuasive writing instruction builds developmentally appropriate foundations on which students may grow and develop the skills they need to be strong persuasive writers. One challenging cornerstone of strong persuasive writing, particularly in argument writing (see *Umbrella* graphic on page 8), is providing credible evidence to back up one's views. This requires students to research sources to help them develop and support their thinking. This often means reading and synthesizing information from a variety of genres and content areas, requiring challenging skills and strategies for students and teachers who may not have strong understandings of how to teach them (Newell et al. 2011, 276). As stated earlier, persuasive writing results tend to be weak in schools (Newell et al. 2011, 276). As a result, plenty of bright college-educated teachers never learned some of the fundamentals of strong persuasive writing. These fundamentals include, but are not limited to, evaluating the strength of an argument, locating relevant sources and determining their credibility, framing an argument with logical reasoning and strong evidence, and addressing and refuting counter-arguments.

The *My View, My Voice* Solution: We have broken the teaching of persuasive writing into a series of developmentally appropriate strategies with examples, explanations, and lesson samples. This will empower teachers to plan the focused instruction, demonstration, and scaffolding that students need to be strong persuasive writers. This book offers 21 strategies and 10 lessons with plenty of explanation and a variety of resources to support them.

2. The scope of the persuasive writing that schools explore is too narrow.

Explanation: Mention persuasive writing to most teachers and students, and it conjures images of dry pencil and paper essays, often five paragraphs in length, focusing on tired, overused topics, such as "Why Smoking Is Bad for You" and "Should Students Wear Uniforms?" Yawn. This instructional rut is largely due to factors such as teachers' limited repertoire of strategies for teaching persuasive writing, "that's how we have always done it" habits, and widespread teaching to the requirements of state tests, which often have a persuasive writing component. School curriculum typically spends so much time focused on this stale, artificial writing, which by the way only exists in schools, that a world of authentic (and engaging) persuasive genres goes largely ignored (Freedman 1996; Newell et al. 2011).

The *My View, My Voice* Solution: *My View, My Voice* broadens the horizons for our persuasive writing students and their teachers. We encourage students to explore a wide variety of real-world genres, media, and purposes for persuasive writing as both readers and writers. It is fine to teach students to write strong essays, but why not also encourage them to analyze and create movie trailers, blog posts, speeches, and posters? This variety is more likely to appeal to students' interests and learning styles, meet the needs of diverse learners, and prepare students to be critical consumers of the many persuasive messages they encounter in their everyday lives.

3. Students are not reading enough persuasive writing.

Explanation: Pam Allyn, director of LitLife, Inc. often says, "Reading is breathing in, and writing is breathing out." Indeed, reading and writing go hand in hand. Reading persuasive text will make your students strong writers of persuasive text (NCTE 2016). Yet, many classrooms do not spend the time they need reading, analyzing, and annotating persuasive texts. Part of the challenge, as stated above, is that the range of persuasive writing that students explore as readers and writers tends to be very limited. Another part of the challenge is that it is hard to find persuasive texts that are appropriate for younger students, particularly at the K–5 level (Biancarosa and Snow 2006, 18).

The *My View, My Voice* Solution: *My View, My Voice* recognizes that in order to become a strong persuasive writer, it is essential to combine explicit writing instruction with strategic reading of persuasive texts (Crowhurst 1990; Newell et al. 2011). Each *My View, My Voice* text provides a sampling of editorials, infographics, advertisements, social media posts, and high-interest topics at varied and appropriate reading levels for teachers and students to analyze and use as models for writing. We also expand the scope of texts that students typically read in school and direct teachers to where to find authentic examples to provide for their students.

4. Authentic engagement in argument requires "arguing."

Explanation: As students build their capacities to develop and support their views, collaboration is key. *Learning to argue* requires *arguing to learn*. Students who engage in collaborative conversations strengthen their abilities to reason and express themselves (Reznitskaya et al. 2007, 449). Many teachers and students, however, have negative associations with the notion of argument. Teachers often value conflict-free zones in their classrooms (Newell 2011) and may worry that conflict will develop into undesirable competition or combativeness that we often see play out in the media (Johnson and Johnson 2009). Students may be afraid to disagree with their teachers and peers (Newell 2011). They may fear being perceived as being disrespectful by the teacher or that others will not like them if they have differing views. They may feel safer going along with the majority or staying silent.

The *My View, My Voice* Solution: *My View, My Voice* encourages teachers and students to recognize the power of conversation when trying to learn about a topic and develop points of view. We prompt them to redefine their attitudes toward argument and recognize the productive value of disagreement in a purposeful, controlled setting. We provide tips for classroom management and scaffolding to keep the conversation going.

Introduction *(cont.)*

5. Teachers are the only people reading students' persuasive writing.

Explanation: The fundamental purpose of the persuasive genre, *to persuade others to believe or do something*, establishes an inextricable connection between the writing and the audience. The very mission of persuasive writers is to influence their audiences in some way. Therefore, students are expected to make compelling points and provide powerful support that will shift the thinking and behavior of...wait...who? Most of the time, no one in particular, except maybe the teacher sitting at her desk with a pile of other similar assignments. That's not very exciting for kids, is it? Yet, when students can identify authentic audiences for their writing, they are more likely to make wise, thoughtful choices about what to include, how to organize the content, and the voice or tone they choose to use (Graham et al. 2012; Crowhurst 1990).

The *My View, My Voice* Solution: *My View, My Voice* establishes the audience as an essential player in the writer-reader relationship right from kindergarten. While simply identifying a theoretical audience is a step in the right direction, we advocate that teachers inject authenticity into their students' writing whenever possible. Authenticity is a magic ingredient that awakens motivation, passion, and attention to quality in young writers. Therefore, we provide suggestions for writing about real reasons to real people to make real change.

The K–8 Continuum

Third, fourth, and fifth grade is a time of exploration and expansion for students. Students at this age are often intensely curious and will energetically explore new topics and research familiar ones as they seek to make sense of the world around them. They continue to seek and value the guidance of their parents and teachers, but they also crave greater levels of independence and autonomy than ever before. They will respond with enthusiasm and engagement when allowed to pursue topics of personal interest and choose how to gather and present information. With modeling and structure, they are ready and able to work productively in groups and on their own.

Students in this age group are widening their view of the world and are increasingly inclined to have strong, often passionate, opinions about issues of importance to them. We see a shift in focus from topics of personal concern (e.g., my favorite foods) to general concern (the impact of pollution on the environment). They are ready to understand and appreciate the importance of facts and information as factors in the development of one's views, and they are beginning to be able to engage in abstract reasoning—an ability that will help them analyze and evaluate the opinions and arguments of others.

Third, fourth, and fifth graders are well equipped and eager to share their views with the world, and we provide tangible and easy-to-implement learning opportunities and strategies to channel their voices, strengthen their stances, listen to the views of others, and cultivate their persuasive techniques when expressing their ideas through both speech and writing. As students advance on their journey with persuasive writing, *My View, My Voice* will provide the developmentally appropriate tools necessary to support teachers and students along the journey.

What does persuasive writing look like across the grades of kindergarten to eighth grade? What is consistent? What shifts across the years? Across all grades, *My View, My Voice* guides students to understand that the primary purpose of persuasive writing is to persuade—to influence the beliefs and behaviors of others—and that this is most effectively done by providing logical reasoning and evidence to support one's views. We encourage students of all grade levels to examine and evaluate the purpose and effectiveness of the persuasive techniques writers use as they explore a wide variety of genres as both readers and writers. We charge all students to find topics that matter to them and motivate them to make a difference by sharing their views in order to persuade others. Across all grades, we teach students to use conversation, collaboration, and information from a variety of sources to support and refine their views.

As students advance up the grade levels, they practice increasingly complex persuasive strategies.

In kindergarten through grade five, students write opinion pieces that present their opinions on a topic and provide relevant reasons and evidence to support their opinions. In grades three to five, they also begin to build skills to identify faulty logic and weak arguments in order to strengthen their own. By grades six to eight, students advance beyond writing opinion pieces to the more sophisticated genre of argument writing. They take stances on arguable issues, and compose arguments that provide reasons based on researched evidence, taking opposing views into account. Students explore detailed protocols to evaluate sources for their evidence and to identify bias.

The ***My View, My Voice* Strategy Continuum Kindergarten to Grade 8** table shown on pages 14–15 provides an overview of the 21 strategies crafted for each grade band. It allows you to see what we expect students to experience now and what we are preparing them for in the future.

Introduction *(cont.)*

The My View, My Voice Strategy Continuum

Kindergarten to Grade 8

	GRADES K–2	GRADES 3–5	GRADES 6–8
1	Writers distinguish between fact and opinion.	Writers explore the relationship between fact and opinion.	Writers discover and explore persuasive writing in the real world.
2	Writers discover and explore persuasive writing in the real world.	Writers discover and explore persuasive writing in the real world.	Writers distinguish between opinion writing and argument writing.
3	Writers consider the impact of characters' opinions in literature.	Writers analyze the elements of persuasive writing.	Writers recognize that an argument can be a positive thing.
4	Writers explore the elements of opinion writing.	Writers examine the techniques that strengthen persuasive writing.	Writers examine the techniques that strengthen persuasive writing.
5	Writers form opinions about topics they know well.	Writers form opinions about issues they care about.	Writers recognize faulty logic in persuasive pieces.
6	Writers form opinions about issues they care about.	Writers consider multiple viewpoints on an issue.	Writers recognize bias.
7	Writers provide reasons for their opinions.	Writers evaluate the strength of reasoning in persuasive pieces.	Writers evaluate the credibility of sources.
8	Writers use conversation to develop their ideas.	Writers recognize faulty logic in persuasive pieces.	Writers evaluate the strength of the argument in persuasive pieces.
9	Writers provide additional information to support reasoning.	Writers use conversation to develop their ideas.	Writers explore the various sides of an issue to identify a claim.
10	Writers try to convince the audience to agree with their opinions.	Writers provide logical reasons to back opinions.	Writers develop sound reasons rooted in evidence.
11	Writers use primary and secondary research to support their opinions.	Writers provide evidence to support reasons.	Writers provide evidence from credible sources to support reasons.

	GRADES K–2	GRADES 3–5	GRADES 6–8
12	Writers add call-to-action messages to their pieces.	Writers use research to gather information to support their opinions.	Writers use original research, interviews, and polls supporting information.
13	Writers plan how they want to respond to their call-to-action statements.	Writers match the evidence to the audience, purpose, and reasoning.	Writers acknowledge and refute counterclaims.
14	Writers use linking words and phrases to connect ideas.	Writers use effective words and phrases to connect ideas.	Writers keep their audience and purpose in mind.
15	Writers choose descriptive words that strengthen their messages.	Writers establish a credible, persuasive voice and tone.	Writers use academic language to express, connect, and clarify ideas.
16	Writers add visual support to strengthen their pieces.	Writers add visual support to express and clarify ideas.	Writers establish a credible, persuasive voice and tone.
17	Writers write structured opinion pieces.	Writers write structured opinion pieces.	Writers add multimedia and visuals to express and clarify ideas.
18	Writers express opinions in a variety of genres.	Writers express opinions in a variety of genres.	Writers write structured argument pieces.
19	Writers revise for publication.	Writers revise for publication.	Writers persuade an audience in a variety of genres.
20	Writers edit for publication.	Writers edit for publication.	Writers revise and edit for publication.
21	Writers publish and share opinions with an authentic audience.	Writers publish and share opinions with an authentic audience.	Writers publish and share opinions with an authentic audience.

Introduction *(cont.)*

Closure

At his 2016 Howard University commencement speech, President Obama spoke about the value of openly listening and learning from the views of others, even when they are not aligned with yours:

> "So, do not try to shut folks out, do not try to shut them down, no matter how much you may disagree with them...Let them talk...That does not mean you should not challenge them. Have the confidence to challenge them, the confidence in the rightness of your position. There will be times when you should not compromise your core values, your integrity, and you will have the responsibility to speak up in the face of injustice. But listen. Engage. If the other side has a point, learn from them. If they're wrong, rebut them. Teach them. Beat them on the battlefield of ideas."
>
> —President Barack Obama *(Howard University Commencement Address)*

The future our students face is a complicated one. As future workers and citizens, students must be equipped with the tools they need to tackle complex issues and engage with others whose ideas may differ significantly from their own. They will need to evaluate the abundance of facts and interpretations available to them in order to shape their own views. Hopefully, they will be ready and willing to use their voices to openly collaborate with others to exchange perspectives that will deepen their own understandings and lead to a path that will move everyone forward.

The urgency to help students build the skills and strategies to analyze, evaluate, and compose opinions and arguments could not be greater. Persuasive writing instruction provides an ideal opportunity to synthesize and strengthen these skills. We hope that the *My View, My Voice* book series will enable teachers and students to engage in persuasive writing with expertise, confidence, and joy.

Questions for Professional Growth

- What types of persuasive writing happen in your classroom right now?
- What strengths do you observe? Where would you like your students to grow?
- What persuasive strategies do you actively model for your students? What might you add to your planning?
- How often do you use reading to build your students' persuasive writing skills? What teaching practices or resources would enhance your students' reading experiences?
- What role does conversation, or arguing to learn, play in helping your students develop and share their views?
- Do your students have opportunities to write about authentic issues for real audiences? How can you inject more authenticity into your students' writing lives?

The Language of Persuasion

"Persuasion is often more effective than force."
—Aesop

Overview

What is the language of persuasion? What words and terms should our third, fourth, and fifth graders know in order to effectively consume, create, and converse about persuasive texts? Students as young as kindergarten are well versed in sharing their favorite facts and opinions and even providing reasons to support their opinions. "Did you know that alligators are carnivores?" "Unicorns are my favorite animal!" "I love bats because they are nocturnal."

Being able to express these thoughts, however, does not mean they know what fact, opinions, and reasons are, unless we provide explicit instruction on those terms. By providing such instruction, teachers help students understand the vocabulary of the persuasive genre that will enable them to think and talk about the key elements they need to notice in their reading and use in their writing.

This section will look closely at the academic language associated with persuasive writing and identify and define some essential terms of the genre. There are also sentence frames and simple activities to help students build their language of persuasion so that they can become familiar with and comfortable using these essential terms. The goal is to encourage teachers and students to use these terms frequently as they discuss persuasive reading and writing. The more teachers and students actively use the terms in real contexts, the more likely the students will retain them as part of their permanent academic vocabulary (Stahl 2005).

The Language of Persuasion *(cont.)*

The list below contains the essential vocabulary that students should become very comfortable with as they are immersed in the persuasive genre. It is recommended that over the course of the school year, the teacher names and notices other terms (see tip box for ideas) encountered. Section 6 provides simplified definitions that may be more suitable for use with grades 3–5 students.

	DEFINITION	EXAMPLE
Audience	the reader or listener who the writer intends to reach or convince	If your audience is other students, create a poster for the cafeteria.
Call to action	a section where the author/speaker prompts the audience to do something	Stop littering and make sure to throw away all your garbage!
Claim	a statement or assertion that something is true	All third graders should be able to choose their own seats in the cafeteria.
Closure or concluding statement or section	a sentence or a section that closes a piece	Since bats are nocturnal and eat mosquitoes, they are very important animals.
Credible	able to be believed; convincing	Anthony provides credible reasons for his opinion. That website is not a credible source because we do not know who published it.
Detail	examples, facts, or additional information that support the point; also called *supporting details*	Alligators are reptiles because they lay eggs and have dry, scaly skin.
Evidence	information that verifies the truth of something; proof; evidence backs a reason	Do you have any evidence that bacon is unhealthy?
Fact	a statement of truth	Alligators are carnivores.
Genre	a type or category of literature	fairy tale, opinion writing, adventure, play
Illustration	a picture or a drawing, often artist-created, used to add meaning, information, or decoration to a book or other written material	
Introduction	the opening statement or section of a piece of writing	We have a problem in our town that needs to be addressed: Lake Cosmo is polluted.
Issue	an important topic or problem	Pollution in Lake Cosmo is a big issue for our town.
Linking words and phrases	words and phrases that join together ideas (e.g., *because, and, also, another*)	I love my dog *because* he is warm and fluffy. *Another* reason fishing is fun is that it is very relaxing.
Logic	a particular way of thinking about something; reasoning	Supurna's mom failed to see the logic of letting her play before finishing her homework.

The Language of Persuasion *(cont.)*

	DEFINITION	EXAMPLE
Opinion	a personal belief; may be true for many, but not true for all	Quinn thinks amusement parks are fun.
Persuasive writing	writing that tries to convince the reader of a specific point of view or to take a specific action	a letter to a grandmother to persuade her to visit
Preference	a greater liking for one choice over another	I like cake better than cookies.
Purpose	the reason something is done or created	I wrote this letter to convince my principal that we need more books in the library.
Reason	a cause or explanation for an opinion; may serve to persuade another to share or change an opinion	It is important for everyone to get exercise because exercise helps us stay healthy.
Reasoning	the careful thinking one does when trying to make a judgment or draw a conclusion; also, the related reasons and evidence one uses to explain and justify a judgment or conclusion	I know Langston thinks we should not have zoos, but what is his reasoning?
Sound reasoning	reasoning that is clear, relevant, and sensible	I think her reasoning is sound because she supports her points with facts.
Source	a book, a resource, a survey, a person, etc., supplying information on a topic	I did research on my topic and used three sources of information in my essay.
Stance	an individual's point of view on an issue with varied opinions	Her stance on students choosing their own seats in the cafeteria is different from that friend's.
Summary of reasoning	a statement or a section, usually in the conclusion of an essay, that concisely sums up the author's main conclusion(s)	In this essay, I have proven that dogs make excellent pets because they are friendly, smart, and helpful.
Tone	the attitude of an author that is conveyed in his or her writing	Raina's anger toward mistreatment of animals is made clear by the tone of her piece. It is important to have a polite tone in your piece because the mayor will read it.
Topic	the main subject of a piece named in a few words	littering, animals, sports
View	a person's way of seeing things based on his or her knowledge and experiences; stance	NieNie thinks the zoo is the best field trip because she loves animals. Dana, however, wants to go to the ballpark because she is a baseball fan.
Voice	the personality of an author that is conveyed by his or her writing	I can really hear Jose's voice coming through in this piece. It sounds just like him.

The Language of Persuasion *(cont.)*

Sentence Frames

The following sentence frames can help develop students' understanding of the essential terms in reading and writing. The teacher can make these sentence frames part of daily teaching. For example, when students turn and talk with partners or need scaffolding composing sentences in writing, encourage them to use the sentence frames to structure their conversations.

Expressing an Opinion

My favorite ______________________ is ______________________, because ______________________ ______________________.

I believe that ______________ since ______________________________.

I am certain that ______________________.

Adding More

What's more, ____.

Furthermore, ____.

Most of all, ____.

Ordering

Then, ____.

Next, ____.

Finally, ____.

Providing Examples

For example, ____.

In this case, ____.

It is obvious that ____.

Concluding

In conclusion, ____.

In summary, ____.

I have argued that ____.

Citing Facts and Evidence

I learned that ______________________. According to ______________ [*state source*] ______________________, ______________________.

Research shows that ____.

The Language of Persuasion *(cont.)*

Tips to Immerse Students in Essential Vocabulary

- Conduct read-alouds and shared reading of persuasive texts, and use these terms to name and notice the elements you encounter.
- Post the terms in the room on laminated cards where both teachers and students can see them. They will serve as reminders to use the terms when reading and writing with students and in relevant classroom discussions. Pull the cards to highlight during a discussion or lesson, and refer to them directly.
- Prompt students to use the terms accurately when they talk about their reading or writing.
- Use sentence frames to help students construct sentences when speaking or writing. Post the list, and refer to the sentence-frame poster for students to use like a menu to scaffold sentence composition.
- Have students create sentence strips to demonstrate how to use the words. Display the sentence strips around the classroom.
- Ask a question that elicits strong opinions and allows students to express their points of view on the issue, such as: *What is the best movie you have ever seen?* Choose sentence frames for students to use in their responses. Model how to share your opinion using a sentence frame. Then, model how to provide reasons to support the opinion also using the sentence frame. Provide students time to share their opinions and reasons using sentence frames.

Questions for Professional Growth

- What teaching do you do to build academic language? What has been successful? What has felt challenging?
- How often do you explicitly teach lessons around building academic language?
- How can you use these sentence frames across the different content areas?
- Instead of alphabetical order, sequence the terms in order from most basic to most sophisticated for your students. Plan how you will introduce the terms gradually for students to use as readers and writers.

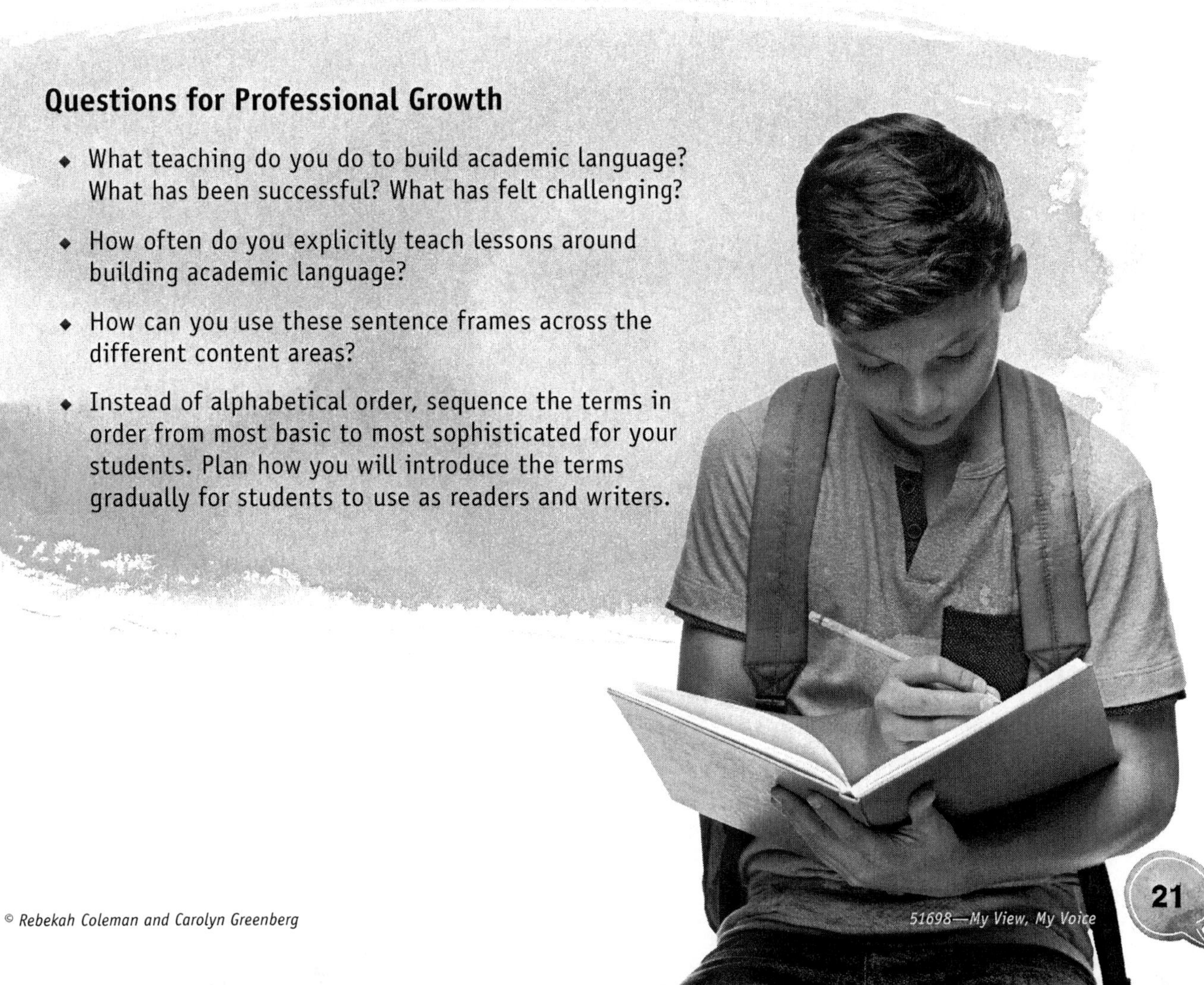

Topic Choice Matters

"Let us remember: One book, one pen, one child, and one teacher can change the world."

—Malala Yousafzai

SECTION 2

Overview

What makes persuasive writing exciting and enticing for many students is that the focus is truly on *their* views. It provides a chance for teachers to say to students: "People care about what you think." "Your views matter." "Your voice and your writing can make a difference in the world in positive, productive ways." "We want to hear what you have to say."

Sure, many students find this kind of recognition and empowerment motivating, but it is important not to put the cart before the horse. Passion is driven by content, but the content has to matter to the students. Before students will be ready to form and share passionate viewpoints and produce powerful writing, teachers must help them find topics that matter to them. This section provides a rationale for allowing students the agency to choose their own topics with the basic elements of strong topic choices for grades 3–5 students. Later, in Section 4, specific strategies are provided for how to support students in choosing topics that will lead to engaging, effective persuasive writing.

Topic Choice Matters *(cont.)*

Understanding the Concept

The first step to strong persuasive writing is a strong persuasive topic. To connect students with strong topics, it is important to help them understand what a topic is. The topic is the main subject of a piece. Typically, the topic of a piece may be named in a few words or less—cafeteria food, television advertisements, *E.T.* the movie, cell phones as a learning tool. Keeping things concise will help students differentiate between *the topic* and *their feelings about the topic.* Why is this important?

Strictly speaking, the topic does not include any opinion, judgment, or stance. Some students may have some difficulty teasing out the difference between the topic and their opinions about the topic. Gentle guidance in understanding the difference between these key elements will help them to understand the concept that different people may have different views on the same topic. Two people may both write about cell phones as a learning tool, but one person's opinion may be that cell phones are important educational tools, whereas the other person may have the opinion that cell phones are a distraction to learning. Understanding that topic and opinion are separate is an important foundation to the concepts that surround argument writing. Below is a sample conversation that demonstrates how a teacher helps a student distinguish between topic and opinion. Distinguishing between such key elements allows students to clarify their thinking and readies them to navigate additional elements, such as reasoning and evidence.

T: What is your topic?

S: I am writing about how I like the old movie *E.T.*

T: So, what is the topic of that piece? Remember not to include your opinion when you tell me.

S: The movie *E.T.*

T: Right! The movie *E.T.* is your topic. What is your opinion of that movie?

S: I think it is a movie everyone should take the time to watch.

T: Wonderful. I cannot wait to hear all your reasons why you think it is such a great movie!

Topic:	**Some examples of topics:**	**The following are not effective ways to name the topics on the left because they do not separate the topic from the author's viewpoint:**
The main subject of a piece. Writers should be able to name the topic in a few words or less. A topic does not contain an opinion, judgment, or stance.	Marc Brown (the author)	My favorite author.
	the beach	I love the beach.
	my cousin Louisa	Louisa is the best cousin.
	cafeteria food	Our cafeteria needs healthier choices.
	our school playground	We need to clean up our school playground.
	skateboards	Skateboarding is a beneficial activity for everyone.

Guidelines for Choosing Topics Effectively

Practically anything is a potential topic for persuasive writing because no matter what the topic is, someone is likely to have an opinion about it. Everyone knows that people have opinions about practically everything! However, not every topic is a strong choice for every writer. Assuming that students understand what a topic is, it is important to consider what makes a topic strong. Four elements of a strong topic for persuasive writing have been identified and briefly explained below.

1. The writer knows about the topic.

Explanation: In order to write persuasively about a topic, it stands to reason that one must first have some knowledge about the topic. The deeper the knowledge is, the better one is able to back an opinion with credible facts and specific examples, which will be more convincing than general statements and pure emotion.

Recommendations for teaching:

- Provide access to a wide range of informational texts on topics (via independent reading and teacher read-alouds) that may interest your students.
- Guide students toward topics about which they have background knowledge, or encourage students to learn about a topic through reading, research, or practical experience whenever possible *before* writing.
- Remind students to use what they have learned as support in their writing. Build a habit of referring to sources when supporting their thinking. "I learned that...." and "According to ______," are helpful stems to frame the conversation. See Section 1 for more support with the language of persuasion.
- Avoid accepting complex topics about which the students know little, if there is no opportunity for them to build their knowledge. When students know a lot about a topic, they will discover that they have a lot to say about it.

2. The writer understands the topic.

Explanation: This condition extends beyond knowing about a topic to whether the student is ready to conceptually understand and process the topic in order to write effectively about it. Many topics are too complex or too disturbing for young students to explore. Building understanding of such topics may be impractical, inappropriate, or even impossible. In addition, students will be unable to write about certain topics with the depth and diplomacy necessary to honor the topic and avoid offending the audience. A fourth grader, for example, may understand conceptually what the death penalty is, yet they would not be developmentally ready to process the information necessary to take an informed stance on the issue.

Recommendations for teaching:

- Grades 3–5 writers are certainly ready to expand their writing horizons from topics of personal importance (e.g., My Favorite Teacher, I Like Pizza, Why Gym Is the Best Subject) to include opinions that address broader issues that impact people other than themselves (Clean Up Our Beach, Save the Bees, Healthy Eating Matters).

Topic Choice Matters *(cont.)*

- Guide students toward topics that are appropriate for their intellectual and emotional development. Avoid topics that are overly complex, controversial, disturbing, or offensive to others.
- If unsure, check a student's conceptual understanding of a topic verbally by engaging them in conversation before tasking them to write about it.
- When one needs to steer a student away from a topic, it is helpful to have a large selection of engaging topics on hand to help him or her choose a new one. Section 4 includes a long list of topics that appeal to this age group. Be sure that *appropriate* is not synonymous with *boring*, which leads to the next guideline.

3. The writer cares about the topic.

Explanation: A writer may know about a topic and understand it well enough to have an opinion, but does the writer care enough about the topic to write well about it? Students will write the most compelling persuasive pieces about topics that spark their interest, stir their emotions, and tap their desires to reach an audience through their writing.

Recommendations for teaching:

- Guide students to gather ideas for topics that are meaningful to them.
- Cultivate a culture in the classroom in which students feel safe to express their opinions.
- Build emotional awareness to help students get in touch with topics that evoke strong feelings, which are often centered around strong opinions. What makes them feel happy, excited, nervous, or fired up?
- Allow students to choose their own topics whenever possible. Kids are usually the best judges of what they care about.
- Prompt student-to-student and teacher-to-student conversation to allow students to explore topics and their feelings about them.
- Honor students' topic choices, and help them develop opinions or take stances on issues related to their topics of interest.
- Let students express their true opinions. If there is only one acceptable point of view on a topic, it is probably not a good topic.

4. The writer has a purpose for writing about the topic.

Explanation: Purpose is an extremely important but elusive condition for strong persuasive writing. What provides a persuasive writer with purpose? An audience who is genuinely interested in the writer's message and a motive to share one's views in order to make a difference in their own life or the lives of others. More often than not, however, students compose persuasive pieces only because they have been assigned to do so. There is no purpose or reward other than a grade. There usually is no audience other than the teacher. Removing purpose from the equation negates the fundamental point of persuasive writing—to persuade!

Topic Choice Matters *(cont.)*

Recommendations for teaching:

- Encourage students to consider the needs of themselves and others (in their class, in their school, in their communities, in the country, and beyond) and ways that they and others can make a difference.
- Brainstorm ways that students can make the world a better place in both small and large ways; center persuasive writing around these ideas.
- When possible, guide students to compose "calls to action" that can actually be realized if one successfully persuades the right audience (e.g., choosing a class pet, homework during summer and winter breaks, building a skate park).
- Frequently refer to "your audience" when speaking to students about their writing. For example, "What do you want your audience to do?" and "What do you need to tell your audience to get them to believe what you are saying?"
- Find genuine ways for students to share their opinions with authentic audiences. Allow students the opportunity to learn that they are not only writing for the teacher but for a much broader audience. Examples may include: creating nooks in the classroom where students can share their opinions on their personal preferences (such as a favorite author or character corner), creating an "our opinions matter" wall with posters or infographics on a range of topics that matter to students, letters to family members, creating a website for a cause, and planning appeals to school and community leaders.

Topic Choice Matters *(cont.)*

Let Students Have Choices

When possible, encourage students to choose their own topics. A student who participates in choosing a topic is more motivated and engaged in the writing (and research) process (Biancarosa and Snow 2006) than when topics are assigned. After all, students are typically the best judges of what matters to them and what inspires them to write. That does not mean that every student starts with a blank sheet of paper and a green light to start writing but rather that teachers provide them with choices within a writing assignment whenever possible.

Choice can come in a variety of forms. For example, rather than simply asking them to write about their opinions of a book they read, teachers may ask them to write about their favorite authors so they get to choose which author they love the most. The entire class may be creating poster advertisements, but the students get to choose which of their favorite games or movies they want to advertise. The class may be charged with the shared writing of a letter to the mayor of your town to persuade him or her to act on issues of their choice. One teacher created a project in which students researched a cause that supported the community in order to write persuasive articles that promoted the cause.

OUR OPINION WRITING TOPICS

Joseph – football
James – dancing
Talia – playing drums
Brian – the beach
Rebekah – reading
Abby – cheese
Mel – her dog Cosmo
Alexander – Legos
Michael – birds
Julia – Harry Potter
Tara – acting

Jack – George Washington
Luis – chocolate
Georgia – mermaids
Patrick C. – wrestling
Patrick J. – Grandma Anita
Jayvon – cars
Laney – squirrels
Noa – horses
Katie – drawing
Cory – carrots
Becky – music

Record students' topic choices on a chart and post it in the classroom for their reference and yours.

One of the realities of having 25 students choose their own topics is that teachers may end up with 25 different topics happening at one time in a writing class. If this is not something one is used to, do not worry. Most of the time, this will go just fine. Writing at this grade level is not usually too overwhelming or in depth in content for a teacher to coach multiple topics effectively, even when research is involved. Much of the time, persuasive writing does not lend itself to a one-size-fits-all topic assignment, anyway. The teacher in the classroom next door is probably not going to have the same favorite author as the principal, and that's a good thing. Students learn when they hear how we all have differing opinions, positions, and ways of backing up those views.

Limited Choice Is Better than No Choice at All

Occasionally, it may be practical or even desirable to provide a limited range of topics from which to choose instead of a wide-open field of possibilities. In these instances, it is recommended that teachers offer students a choice, if at all possible, but direct them to choose from a list of teacher-selected choices. With some structure and training, students will be able to work in small teams to research the same topic together and then either compose a single piece of writing or individual ones.

Some reasons to provide limited choice of topics are:

- **To compare views on the same topic.** Understanding that different people may have different opinions on the same topic is a key concept to develop in persuasive writing.
- **Students need to focus on topics that are required by local curriculum.** Perhaps the curriculum has content objectives that lend themselves to persuasive writing. By all means, take the opportunity to make cross-disciplinary connections. Try to provide a few options within the larger curricular topic. For example, the topic may be the book being read aloud, but should provide students the option to write about the main character, the author, the illustrator, or a specific page.
- **There are not enough resources for students to research separate topics.** In this case, it may help to gather resources on four or five topics and have students choose from those.

When Topic Choice Is Not Possible

Sometimes, curricular materials, local or standardized assessments, and other situations may present instances where students must write to a common prompt, especially as they advance through the grades and formal writing assessment becomes more prevalent. This can be daunting for students and teachers alike, especially when students must write about topics about which they have little knowledge or interest. Well-written prompts should be on topics that are universal to all students' experiences, but in reality, not all prompts turn out to be equally suitable for all students.

If a single prompt is not appropriate for one or more students, adjust it to suit their experience or needs. The teacher should decide whether that makes sense and if it is within his or her control to do so. Sometimes, particularly on standardized texts, it is not possible to change a prompt that may not feel like a good match for students. Since this is likely to happen many times during their school careers, consider it a good experience for them to learn how to face this situation. If students are feeling anxious about a prompt, be positive and reassure them that they are well-prepared writers and should trust their instincts.

Questions for Professional Growth

- What are the benefits of allowing students to choose their own persuasive topics?
- How often do your students have the opportunity to choose their own topics?
- Where do you have opportunities to promote more topic choices for your students?
- Where is topic choice not practical or possible? How can you build students' confidence and engagement in these situations?

Many Ways of Writing

"The function of education is to teach one to think intensively and to think critically. Intelligence plus character—that is the goal of true education."

—Martin Luther King Jr.

Overview

This book broadly defines persuasive writing as any text created with the purpose of persuading others. A writer's ideas may appear in many forms, such as traditional essays, infographics, posters, or advertisements. The message may be handwritten, drawn, spoken aloud, created on a computer, and more.

Frequently, persuasive writing is taught through traditional assignments such as opinion essays, editorials, and book reviews. There is value in these traditional pieces because they encourage students to learn the elements and structure of persuasive writing and provide a useful vessel for organizing their thinking. Moreover, most educational standards and many tests require that students learn how to write in these traditional forms. Therefore, students will continue to practice these types of writing in Section 4.

Teachers can expand beyond the traditional forms and explore the types of persuasive writing encountered in the "real" world. These include advertisements, political speeches, blogs and social-media posts, infographics, posters, movie trailers, travel brochures, and more. This will allow students to build repertoires of engaging and dynamic persuasive-writing assignments and sharpen their abilities to engage with persuasive texts in the real world.

Writing in a variety of persuasive writing forms also allows students to practice writing for multiple purposes and audiences. A letter may appeal to a school or a community leader. An informational poster may raise an important issue with the neighbors. A speech may outline the action steps needed to make a positive change in people's behavior. These types of writing require a range of skills and strategies to plan, create, and present. Indeed, research shows that students who write for multiple purposes and audiences in a range of genres and forms become stronger writers (Graham et al. 2012). Providing students with a diversity of experiences will naturally require a broader set of writing techniques, critical-thinking skills, and content knowledge than the ubiquitous five-paragraph school essay. Creating alternative forms of persuasive writing also taps a variety of learning styles. Every classroom has a mélange of artists and poets, introverts and extroverts, actors and athletes. Persuasive writing provides potential opportunities for all types of learners. This section provides a wide variety of suggestions and samples of alternative forms of persuasive writing that we hope will tap students' natural abilities and expand their writing horizons.

Many Ways of Writing *(cont.)*

Reading to Write: The Importance of Reading to Immerse Students in Persuasive Writing

Reading and writing go hand in hand. For students to become strong persuasive writers, they must examine examples of strong persuasive writing through reading. This may happen through teacher read alouds, shared reading, small-group instruction, and independent reading experiences. Through reading, students learn many important lessons, such as the sound of persuasive language, structure and organization, and the conventional rules of the English language. The discussions that accompany reading experiences can build understanding of complex concepts and strategies, such as author's purpose and word choice, the use of visuals to support ideas, the role of audience, and the strength and success of a persuasive message. Students need to have access to a range of persuasive writing through direct instruction as well as availability around the room and in the classroom library. Sometimes, finding age- and level-appropriate persuasive texts across a wide range of genres can be challenging, particularly in grades K–5, so there are original pieces included in Section 6 to help.

TEACHING TIP

Bring in newspapers, magazines, catalogs, and even board game covers. Together, look for, read, and analyze the persuasive messages that abound in these publications. This can be especially fun with messages that are meant to reach students. Rich examples may be found in reviews, advertisements, descriptions of products, letters to the editor, infographics, feature articles, and more. Below is a list of favorite websites for students to use when searching for a range of persuasive messages. See the suggestions for searching with Google and other informational source ideas in the table below.

OUR FAVORITE INFORMATIONAL WEBSITES

Visit these sites for various examples of persuasive pieces.

WEBSITE	CONTENT
Amazon.com (book, movie, game reviews)	Search for book, movie, toy reviews, and customer commentary (strong opinions!).
CommonSenseMedia.org	Watch movie trailers and reviews.
DogoBooks.com	Find book reviews for and by kids.
DogoMovies.com	Find movie reviews and trailers of G, PG, and PG-13 movies.
DogoNews.com	Find current events and news articles on age-appropriate and relevant topics.

Many Ways of Writing *(cont.)*

WEBSITE	CONTENT
EnchantedLearning.com	Find information on a wide range of topics.
Images.Google.com *We recommend that teachers search and select examples in advance in case some material is not suitable for children.	Find a wide variety of persuasive images to analyze by searching categories such as advertisements for children, vintage food advertisements, candy or toy advertisements, infographics for children, persuasive posters, environmental posters.
Google News Archive	Find free access to scanned archives of multiple newspapers dating back to the 1700s; great primary source resource.
HowStuffWorks.com	Find videos, podcasts, and articles on just about every topic.
Kidsdiscover.com/infographics	Find a variety of infographics on a range of topics. **Note:** Infographics need to be selected by teachers to ensure age appropriateness.
KidsHealth.org	Find wide variety of health and body articles, videos, and other features for kids.
Kids.NationalGeographic.com	Find interactive information and videos on animals and places in the world.
KidsKnowIt.com	Find information, podcasts, and videos on a wide range of topics.
magazines.scholastic.com	Find daily news and current events on many relevant topics.
Newsela.com	Find a wide variety of informational and persuasive articles, text sets, and more.
OurLittleEarth.com	Search an international current events newspaper created for kids.
Reading A-Z.com	Find downloadable leveled books, some of which are free, others require a subscription.
Readworks.org	Read leveled reading passages, including informational topics.
SIKids.com	Find sports news articles and videos for kids.
Slimekids.com	Find book and game reviews and book trailers, many of which are written by children.
Spaghettibookclub.org	Read book reviews written by children.

Many Ways of Writing *(cont.)*

WEBSITE	CONTENT
TeachingKidsNews.com	up-to-date news articles for kids with curriculum connection suggestions
TimeforKids.com	age-appropriate articles and reviews on a wide range of informational topics
TTPM.com	TTPM stands for Toys, Tots, Pets and More; engaging reviews for all categories
TweenTribune.com	informational and persuasive articles on a variety of topics K–12; same article provided on several reading levels
The Washington Post for Kids	news articles for kids; printable options
The Why Files Archives	archives of science-related articles on a variety of themes
Wonderopolis.org	engaging informational pieces on a wide variety of topics

SECTION 3

Questions for Professional Growth

- How can you create authentic opportunities for students to share their opinions with others in their school or communities?
- What persuasive forms of writing have you engaged students with?
- What innovative or traditional persuasive forms of writing do you hope to introduce to your students?

Traditional and Innovative Forms of Persuasive Writing

For all of the reasons mentioned above, have students read and write in a wide variety of persuasive forms. Here are some favorite age-appropriate traditional and innovative writing forms.

- **advertisements**
- **book, poem, and movie recommendations; blurbs, trailers**
- **bumper stickers**
- **campaign posters and materials**
- **commercials**
- **contest entries**
- **critiques**
- **debates**
- **editorials and letters to the editor**
- **essays and paragraph writing**
- **feature articles**
- **greeting cards**
- **infographics**
- **job applications (e.g., classroom job application)**
- **pantomime**
- **persuasive letters**
- **persuasive posters and murals**
- **persuasive slide show presentations (PowerPoint, KeyNote, Prezi)**
- **poetry**
- **public announcements**
- **reviews (movies, books, poems, restaurants, stories, toys, etc.)**
- **role playing**
- **songs/jingles/raps**
- **speeches**
- **T-shirt messages**
- **top 10 lists**
- **travel brochures**
- **TV and radio commercials**
- **websites**

SECTION 3

Many Ways of Writing *(cont.)*

High- and Low-Tech Suggestions

While there are often discussions about the benefits and distractions of technology in the classroom, technology is here to stay. Moreover, technology can and does help students become better writers for a variety of audiences and provides many different ways to write for a range of purposes, including persuasion (Gerber and Price 2011).

PURPOSE	HIGH-TECH/LOW-TECH OPTIONS
Create an advertisement for your product, destination, or organization.	**High tech:** Write and rehearse a script, and use a phone or a video recorder to create an audio or video recording of the advertisement. **Low tech:** Write and rehearse a script, and perform it in front of the class.
Create a movie or book trailer.	**High tech:** Write a storyboard for a movie or a book trailer using Storyboard That or Popplet, and use a phone or a video to record the presentation. **Low tech:** Handwrite storyboards, and present them to the class or a broader audience.
Share opinion or public service announcement on a specific topic by creating an infographic.	**High tech:** Use a tool like www.easel.ly.com or www.glogster.com to create an infographic on the topic. Even standard word-processing programs will work using the shapes and table features. **Low tech:** Handwrite an infographic using paper and art supplies.
Share author or illustrator recommendations.	**High tech:** Create a digital book or presentation of student's author and illustrator recommendations that you can share with the class and families or school community via email, using PowerPoint or KeyNote. **Low tech:** Create a class book with opinion paragraphs of author or illustrator recommendations.
Share an opinion on a topic by writing/giving a speech.	**High tech:** Write a speech, and record himself or herself giving the speech; upload it to a class website or private YouTube channel to share with families. **Low tech:** Write a speech, and read it aloud to an authentic audience.
Create a persuasive poster and share with an authentic audience.	**High tech:** Use PowerPoint, Microsoft Word, Glogster, KeyNote, or another presentation website or app to create a persuasive poster on a topic. Create an online slide show of photos of the posters, and share through a classroom blog or website. **Low tech:** Create a handmade poster using art supplies, and set up information stations around the room with displays of persuasive posters; invite families or members of the school community in to learn about the topic.

Many Ways of Writing *(cont.)*

PURPOSE	HIGH-TECH/LOW-TECH OPTIONS
Create a travel brochure for a place you are studying.	**High tech:** Create a travel brochure using Pages, and include maps and images that students find online. **Low tech:** Create a handmade travel brochure using print or hand-drawn maps and images. Display on a wall in the classroom.
Create a podcast of a top 10 list.	**High tech:** Write a top 10 list on a specific topic, and record a podcast using a voice-recording device to post on your class website, or use a platform such as Voicethread.com to record and publish students' writing. **Low tech:** Write a top 10 list on a specific topic, and share the list with the class.
Share a review of a restaurant, a movie, a video game, or a store.	**High tech:** Write a feature article, and publish it on a class blog, such as Kidblog.org, or on a class website. **Low tech:** Write a feature article, and include hand-drawn illustrations and images; create a class book of the reviews of restaurants and stores.
Share opinions concisely after a read aloud, a movie viewing, a field trip, etc.	**High tech:** Use a site such as Todaysmeet.com to create a "backchannel" where students can share opinions in 140 characters or fewer via any computer or mobile device. **Low tech:** Have students express their opinions and reasoning on sticky notes and post them on a board.

Promoting Strong Persuasive Writing

"Although I'm only fourteen, I know quite well what I want. I know who is right and who is wrong. I have my opinions, my own ideas and principles, and although it may sound pretty mad from an adolescent, I feel more of a person than a child. I feel quite independent of anyone."

—Anne Frank

SECTION 4

Overview

The primary goal of this book is to help teachers help students become *effective* and *independent* consumers and composers of persuasive writing. Students can successfully demonstrate their expertise in both classroom and real-world contexts and ultimately possess persuasive skill sets that will benefit them in their careers and personal lives. For this to happen, students need to build confidence and competence with a variety of high-utility persuasive-writing strategies. The strategies selected ensure that when students want to use their own ideas to persuade others or when they need to think critically about the persuasive messages of others, they will confidently know what to do and how to do it.

This section includes 21 strategies that will establish foundations on which students can build as they develop increasingly sophisticated expertise in persuasive writing. (See **21 Persuasive-Writing Strategies for Grades 3–5 Students** on page 41.) Each strategy includes a rationale, an explanation, and resources to help teachers plan. In Section 5, we include model lessons for 10 of the strategies to help teachers visualize how teaching of each strategy might go.

The goal of these strategies is simple—to provide students with a toolbox of strategies that build on each other to support their growth as strong persuasive writers. To support this, a sample unit of study framework is provided in Section 6. There is the freedom to teach opinion writing outside the literacy block, for example as a part of the science curriculum or history curriculum. In this case, choose a specific genre (e.g., an infographic about wildlife or a travel brochure for a place being studied), and then teach the necessary strategies to meaningfully support the project, such as discover and explore persuasive writing in the real world, form opinions about things they know and care about, use conversation to develop their ideas, provide logical reason(s) to back up opinions, provide explanations and evidence to support reasoning, and use research, interviews, and polls to gather supporting information.

Promoting Strong Persuasive Writing *(cont.)*

Supporting Diverse Readers and Writers

The strategies and methods suggested here are purposefully rigorous and challenging. Some of these approaches are more commonly found in middle grades or even higher. Plus, most classes are a diverse group that includes students working well below grade level or at early levels of English language development. Have faith that all students can apply these strategies on a level that is developmentally appropriate for them as individuals. Be open to the fact that success will not look the same for everyone. Nor should it. Keep an eye on the prize, which is for students to build important conceptual foundations and confidently engage in meaningful practice as readers, writers, listeners, and speakers around the art of persuasion. It is important not to water down expectations for higher-level thinking. Assume that students are capable of thinking deeply and profoundly, and persuading others with passion and finesse. Find ways to help students achieve this no matter where on the literacy-learning continuum they currently reside. Keep paying attention to where they are, and move them forward bit by bit. Use the differentiation strategies that accompany the lessons. In addition, here are some general accommodations that can be provided to help students achieve higher levels of literacy:

- Read texts aloud.
- Allow partner reading.
- Provide recorded texts.
- Have students draw their ideas.
- Have students add details to their illustrations (not just to their sentences).
- Have students speak their ideas.
- Have students dictate their ideas.
- Use drawing and talk to prepare for writing.
- Allow developmental spelling.
- Accept variety in the volume of writing students produce.
- Include some genres that are not text heavy.
- Allow students to speak and write in their home languages when possible.

Students' approximations should be celebrated just as the early musical attempts of a middle-school band would be. Perfection is not the goal; learning what musicians do and making music together is. They may not be ready for Carnegie Hall yet, but they are making progress on the journey to get there, and it is important to honor and value that.

Promoting Strong Persuasive Writing *(cont.)*

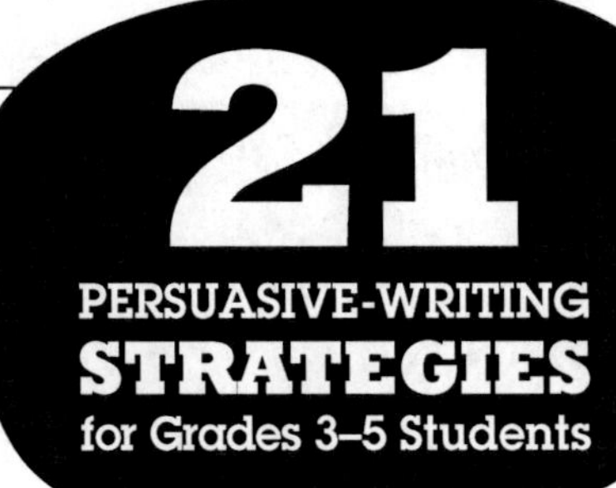

1. Writers explore the relationship between fact and opinion.*
2. Writers discover and explore persuasive writing in the real world.
3. Writers analyze the elements of persuasive writing.*
4. Writers examine the techniques that strengthen persuasive writing.*
5. Writers form opinions about issues they care about.
6. Writers consider multiple viewpoints on an issue.*
7. Writers evaluate the strength of reasoning in persuasive pieces.*
8. Writers recognize faulty logic in persuasive pieces.
9. Writers use conversation to develop their ideas.*
10. Writers provide logical reasons to back up opinions.
11. Writers provide evidence to support reasons.*
12. Writers use research to support their opinions.
13. Writers match the evidence to the audience, purpose, and reasoning.
14. Writers use effective words and phrases to connect ideas.*
15. Writers establish a credible, persuasive voice and tone.*
16. Writers add visual support to express and clarify ideas.
17. Writers write structured opinion pieces.*
18. Writers express opinions in a variety of genres.
19. Writers revise for publication.
20. Writers edit for publication.
21. Writers publish and share opinions with an authentic audience.

* = Model Lesson Included in Section 5

Strategies for Success

Strategy 1: Writers explore the relationship between fact and opinion.

EXPLANATION

It is common practice for K–2 teachers to help students establish a foundation in persuasive writing by learning the difference between fact and opinion. By grade 3, many students have indeed begun to understand the difference between the two even if they still get confused. Once this is the case, students are also ready to begin to understand the roles that fact and opinion play in persuasive writing. Many students regard fact and opinion as opposites of each other. Students also tend to define the associated genres (informational writing and persuasive writing) in overly simplified ways: informational writing contains *facts*, persuasive writing contains *opinions*. In reality, it is not that simple, and grades 3–5 students are ready to begin to consider why it can be challenging to distinguish fact from opinion and explore the relationship between the two when trying to persuade others.

Strong persuasive writing rarely contains opinion only. One of the most common and effective ways to convince others that one's opinion is believable is by providing relevant facts to back it up. That is not to say that opinions are not at all valuable. An opinion from a credible expert can be a very convincing influence. Skilled persuasive writers understand this and use both opinion and facts thoughtfully to persuade others to agree with their views.

SUPPORT FOR THE STRATEGY

1. Make sure that students have a basic understanding of the difference between fact and opinion. Clearly define each for students.

   Fact: a statement of truth. Everyone can agree that a fact is the truth.

   Example: Alligators are animals.

   Opinion: a personal belief. An opinion may be true for many but not true for all people.

   Example: Pizza tastes great.

2. Have a student state a fact (or an opinion). Other students should identify the statement as fact or opinion and provide proof of their thinking.

3. Read or review persuasive texts with students, such as editorials, feature articles, advertisements, or infographics (see Section 3 for more suggestions). Direct students to identify the opinions presented as well as any facts that may be included. Some questions:
   - What is the topic or issue?
   - What is the author's opinion(s) related to the topic? How do you know?
   - Does the author include facts? How do the facts help the author prove his point?
   - Which things does the author say that can be proven to be true? Which things are arguable?

Promoting Strong Persuasive Writing *(cont.)*

4. Help students recognize opinion clue words.
   - Superlatives (*–est* words) like *best, easiest, hardest*, etc., often signal opinions.
   - Descriptive words that require someone to make a personal judgment (*pretty, cute, scary, fun*, etc.) are more likely to form opinion statements. **Note:** Words that describe quantity and visible attributes, such as colors, size, and texture, are more likely to appear in statements of fact.
   - Phrases that signal a person is sharing an opinion (*In my opinion, I think*, etc.).
5. Sometimes, students perceive facts and factual writing as more important or more legitimate than opinion writing. Eliminate the myth that facts are good and opinions are bad. In the real world, most writing is actually opinion writing, even among pieces which would be technically classified as informational writing. This is largely because writing with a personal perspective is more interesting to readers. A completely objective biography of Martin Luther King Jr. would be very dry without the author's view of how he lived and overcame the challenges in his life. Today, the basic facts on practically any topic are available with a quick Internet search. It is an author's opinion on a topic that makes the writing engaging.
6. Emphasize the importance of supporting one's views with both facts *and* opinions. Up-to-date information from credible sources is very compelling. Writers also support their opinions with—yes, opinions! Opinions from experts on a topic go a long way to strengthen one's point. Have students analyze a piece that contains both, highlighting facts in one color and opinions in the other. When students compose their own writing, remind them that sometimes, experts may be found very nearby. For example, in an opinion piece on updating the technology in the library, the school librarian and the students who go to the library are knowledgeable experts on the topic.

Promoting Strong Persuasive Writing *(cont.)*

Strategy 2: Writers discover and explore persuasive writing in the real world.

EXPLANATION

Students need to become wise and critical consumers of the persuasive messages they encounter that try to steer how people spend, travel, vote, eat, work, play, and so on. This begins by helping students become aware of the many forms of persuasive writing in the world and teaching them to understand and analyze how others try to influence them. This will also help them learn how people persuade others and draw from this knowledge when creating persuasive writing of their own. While immersing students in this genre, model how to recognize authentic persuasive writing, and provide clear steps for how to carefully read or listen to analyze the persuasive elements or techniques.

SUPPORT FOR THE STRATEGY

1. Using the Traditional and Innovative Forms of Persuasive Writing list on page 35 as a menu, create an anchor chart of persuasive texts that are familiar to students. Use this as a reference when choosing and discussing texts with the students.

2. Bring in examples of opinion texts that students may relate to in their lives (examples may include newspaper ads, travel brochures, etc.), and ask students to do the same. In addition to written texts, include audio-visual texts, such as TV and radio ads and jingles, movie trailers, political speeches and cartoons, and infographics.

3. Model how to read, view, and listen to persuasive pieces. Some useful questions include:
    - What is the topic of the piece?
    - What is the writer's opinion?
    - What reasons does the writer use to support his or her opinion?
    - What evidence does the writer use to support his or her opinion?
    - Does the writer use facts or opinions to back up his or her main point? How?
    - What is the writer trying to persuade us to believe or do?
    - Does the writer use pictures or other visuals to support his or her thinking? How?

4. Take students around the school to look for persuasive writing. Look for posters, advertisements, directions, etc., that feature opinions and attempt to influence the beliefs or behavior of the viewer (e.g., a poster in the cafeteria about the importance of healthy eating).

5. Compile a collection of texts that are appropriate for the age and reading levels of students to include in the classroom library for independent reading.

6. When choosing texts for group or independent reading, do not exclude those that are mainly or entirely visual—students need to learn to read photos, drawings, and other informational graphics. Review the definition of opinion writing: pieces that express an opinion.

7. Persuasion is a real-world skill! Start a Persuasion Box in the classroom (like a Suggestion Box with a persuasive spin). Invite students to make suggestions, but require them to use reasons and evidence to back up their ideas.

8. Once students are comfortable with the elements of persuasive writing, use the Reading Opinion Writing graphic organizer below. Have students discuss and write about a variety of texts.

Promoting Strong Persuasive Writing *(cont.)*

READING OPINION WRITING

Title:

Type of opinion text:

Topic of opinion text:

Opinion expressed in text:

What I found interesting:

SECTION 4

Promoting Strong Persuasive Writing *(cont.)*

Strategy 3: Writers analyze the elements of persuasive writing.

EXPLANATION

This strategy helps students recognize that common elements occur in many types of persuasive writing. In grades 3–5, we focus on four key elements: *topic*, *opinion*, *reasons*, and *evidence*. Students are provided with the opportunity to examine a variety of texts that differ in form and content from one another but feature these common elements.

SUPPORT FOR THE STRATEGY

1. Be sure students start with a foundational understanding of fact and opinion. See Strategy 1.
2. Teach students to describe the topic of a piece without including the writer's opinion. The topic is the main subject of a piece. Typically, the topic of a piece may be named in a few words. Strictly speaking, the topic does not include any opinion, judgment, or stance. Key understanding: different people may have different views on the same topic. This can be a tricky task depending on the text and students' background knowledge on a topic (Section 2).
    - Choose a sample piece for modeling, such as *Zoos: Good for Animals and People* (page 138). Model how to tease the topic (*zoos*) from the author's opinion. (*Zoos are good for animals and people.*) Provide students with other examples of texts to identify the topic of each.
3. Teach students to recognize opinion clue words (Strategy 1). Using the sample text, *Zoos: Good for Animals and People*, model how to use the words from the graphic on page 43 to find opinion words in the text. Highlight the words. Then, send students on an opinion-word scavenger hunt! They can use the sample texts in Section 6 or real-world examples of persuasive texts (see Section 3).
4. Teach students that the term *claim* is a specific type of opinion. A claim is often used when there are multiple views on a topic. In other words, the writer's stance is up for debate. *I love ice cream* is simply an opinion statement. Not everyone loves ice cream, but no one can really argue that the writer does not love it. *Ice cream is the best dessert in the world* is a claim. Not everyone agrees that this statement is true. There is potential for argument, and given some people's passion for desserts, it may be a heated one!
5. In some texts, opinion must be inferred. This is especially true with advertisements and other texts that rely mainly on visual information. Use this formula as a tool for inferring:

clues in the text + background knowledge = inference

For example, a cartoon depicting Earth with a face that looks ill may not include words that mention pollution or the environment, but students can use their background knowledge to determine the topic and the author's view about it.

SECTION 4

Promoting Strong Persuasive Writing *(cont.)*

Questions for Readers

- What is the topic?
- What is the main opinion (or claim) of the piece?
- What is one reason the writer provides to support the opinion?
- What evidence does that writer provide to prove the reason to be true?

Questions for Writers

- What is the topic?
- What is your opinion (or claim)?
- What is one reason you feel that way?
- What evidence can you provide that can help prove that?

6. As students begin to explore more complex texts, there will be need to distinguish between the main opinion on the topic and other opinions that may be included in the text. The fourth row in the Analyzing Opinion Writing graphic organizer (page 112) makes it clear that students should be searching for the main opinion. Students should understand that other opinions may also be included as part of the reasons and evidence that support the main opinion.

7. Students are ready to build the understanding that reasons and evidence are not exactly the same thing, though they are often intertwined and described under the common umbrella of reasoning or the thought process behind an opinion. Reasons support an opinion but are based on the writer's conclusions and do not necessarily offer proof. Evidence comes from sources that help to prove the reason is true, thus strengthening the opinion statement.

   Opinion: a personal belief

   Reason: a cause or explanation for an opinion; logical support

   Evidence: information that backs up a reason by verifying it; proof

8. Share different examples of persuasive texts (see Section 6), modeling how to identify the elements of opinion writing using the Questions for Readers chart. For support implementing this strategy, use the accompanying lesson found in Section 5.

9. Using the Analyzing Opinion Writing graphic organizer, model how to use the opinion piece to complete the graphic organizer. Have students use the organizer to discuss and write about a variety of texts.

Promoting Strong Persuasive Writing *(cont.)*

Strategy 4: Writers examine the techniques that strengthen persuasive writing.

EXPLANATION

Strategy 4 focuses on sharpening students' awareness of three classic persuasive techniques to persuade one's audience, first described by Aristotle: ethos, pathos, and logos. For example, an advertiser trying to convince a child to buy a new toy wants to generate a sense of excitement (pathos) about the toy. You will also present them with a source they may believe as credible (ethos), such as another kid being super happy with the toy. Finally, you will present them with facts (logos), such as, "It is the best-selling toy nationwide." It is up to the consumer to decide whether the reasoning is sound (which is addressed in Strategy 7), but creators of persuasive texts usually use a combination of these techniques to convince others of their claims.

SUPPORT FOR THE STRATEGY

1. In order for this strategy to fully make sense to students, they must develop a conceptual understanding of *audience*. This will also build a key foundational understanding for students' work as persuasive writers. Do this by:
    - Discussing the purpose of persuasive writing—to convince the audience (e.g., the reader).
    - Explaining that persuasive writers think about who may be interested in their topics or who could make a difference with their issues. They write with that person or group in mind.
    - When conferring with students as they read and write persuasive text, refer to the audience or reader often. This may sound like "How do you think the author wanted readers to react to this photo?"
2. Introduce ethos, pathos, and logos. See page 49 for a student-friendly representation.
3. Discuss what it means to be credible. Together with students' input, create the chart to the right that depicts qualities that contribute to one's credibility.
4. Provide examples for students of how they can recognize ethos, pathos, and logos as both consumers and composers of persuasive text. Page 49 provides general examples to support teachers in explaining these concepts. See page 118 for a simpler, more student-friendly book/chart for students to use as reference when reading or writing persuasive text.

SECTION 4

Promoting Strong Persuasive Writing *(cont.)*

1. Give them a reason to believe you or your source.

Describe your or your source's experience with the topic.

- Mention how you or your source acquired the information you are sharing.
- Mention how you or your source is an expert on the topic.

Ethos

2. Stir the emotion of your audience.

Talk about your feelings about the topic.

- Talk about how the audience feels about the topic.
- Include an illustration or photo that stirs emotions.
- Share an emotional story or image.
- Write or speak with an emotional tone.
- Use loaded language (e.g., *emotional verbs* and *adjectives*).
- Make people feel a part of a group.

Pathos

SECTION 4

3. Use facts and logic.

Add relevant observations you have made yourself.

- Add something you have learned by interviewing or polling others.
- Add facts and statistics you have learned from research. Numbers are especially powerful.
- Add quotes and opinions from experts on the topic.
- Use examples that the audience can relate to their life experiences.

Logos

Promoting Strong Persuasive Writing *(cont.)*

Strategy 5: Writers form opinions about issues they care about.

EXPLANATION

Writing about issues of importance goes hand in hand with trying to persuade others to agree with one's views and possibly take some kind of action. Having an impact on others is the fundamental purpose of persuasive writing.

Guide grades 3–5 students to develop opinions and reasoning related to more outwardly focused topics that matter to them—the writer knows about the topic, the writer understands the topic, the writer cares about the topic, and the writer has a purpose for writing about the topic.

At the same time, we encourage students to become increasingly aware of the opinions of others because issues that matter to a community of people are more likely to generate opposing ideas about which people feel passionate. This engagement with *arguable* issues, in contrast to personal opinions that do not really impact anyone but the opinion-holder, will provide a foundation for students' future work with persuasive writing in upper grades.

SUPPORT FOR THE STRATEGY

1. Use a chart such as the one below to anchor a discussion about widening the scope of topics about which students have views.
2. As the rings on the chart below expand from the center out, notice how the topics change from the personal, self-oriented topics in the center to broader issues that impact many people. See Step 3 for more information about how to write increasingly broad issues.

3. The opinion chart on page 51 articulates the difference between personal, self-oriented opinions and opinions about broader issues.
4. Choose an issue that affects the students' community, such as a problem that needs to be solved or a plan that is going to happen soon. Some discussion questions:
   - What do you think should happen? Why?
   - Do you agree with what is going on? Why, or why not?
   - Would anyone else feel differently? What may his or her view be?

SECTION 4

Promoting Strong Persuasive Writing *(cont.)*

Opinions of Personal Importance	Opinions that Address Broader Issues
Use these ideas to inspire writing about one's personal preferences and beliefs. The goal of such writing is to share a personal opinion and reasons for it. The writer may provide reasons to explain the opinion, but there is little or no expectation to persuade an audience to change its beliefs or behaviors. Others may or may not agree, but there is usually no authentic motivation or effort to persuade others to change their views. Students may form opinions around: ◆ likes (*I like ice cream.*) ◆ dislikes (*I do not like winter.*) ◆ favorites (*Uncle Andy is my favorite uncle.*) ◆ description that requires judgment (amazing, boring, fun, scary, interesting, etc.) (*Halloween is a scary holiday.*) ◆ superlatives (best, worst, funniest, scariest, etc.) (*Gym is the most exciting class.*)	Use these ideas to inspire writing about issues that affect people and situations other than the author. The goal of such writing is to present a strong claim and support for that claim in order to persuade the audience to change its thinking or behavior and possibly take action. There are usually multiple views centered around an issue. Students may form opinions around: ◆ how to change a situation or solve a problem (*We need to clean the park.*) ◆ whether something should happen (*Our class should get a goldfish.*) ◆ evaluation of responses to a situation (*The school should not ban riding scooters.*) ◆ strong feelings about issues that impact a community or the environment (*Everyone should work together to help save bees.*) ◆ strong feelings about how people should act (*Always be kind to everyone in your class.*)

SECTION 4

5. Look at the social studies and science curriculum for inspiration for writing topics and to promote cross-disciplinary connections. Are you supposed to study neighborhoods? Laws? The environment? These real contexts provide a lot of opportunity for developing a viewpoint on a related issue and writing persuasively about it.

6. When students form opinions about broader issues, encourage them to gather more information about the topics. For example, they may feel strongly that the school should not have removed the tire swing, but a talk with the principal may reveal that someone was injured.

7. Teach students to investigate topics respectfully when involving other people. Role-play how a conversation may go. "Principal Jones, I am writing an opinion piece about the tire swing. I am wondering whether you can please tell me more about why we removed it."

8. As students broaden their focus to address topics that impact others, it becomes vital to discuss the importance of being sensitive to others' feelings and presenting one's views with kindness and respect.

Promoting Strong Persuasive Writing *(cont.)*

Strategy 6: Writers consider multiple viewpoints on an issue.

EXPLANATION

As grades 3–5 persuasive writers shift to broader issues in Strategy 5, they will inevitably discover that not everyone sees eye to eye on any given issue. The presence of disagreement, in fact, is embedded in the very definition of the word *issue*—a topic of popular interest about which there are multiple viewpoints. This strategy begins a shift toward "arguing to learn"—using group discussion to share opinions and reasoning and respond to and learn from the thinking of others. While whole-class discussion led by the teacher is a good starting point, we encourage you to move students to peer-to-peer discussions in small groups of two or more as soon as possible. This increases engagement in the talk and builds the important capacity of participating in academically oriented conversation with purpose and independence.

SUPPORT FOR THE STRATEGY

1. Help students establish some essential understandings about disagreement. Two possible ways to approach this: Present this chart as a True or False quiz to spark discussion. Or, ask students some focus questions such as: *Are disagreements ever a good thing? or Do you ever change your mind when you disagree with someone? Why?* Then, use their discussions to expand their thinking and develop some common understandings about arguments.

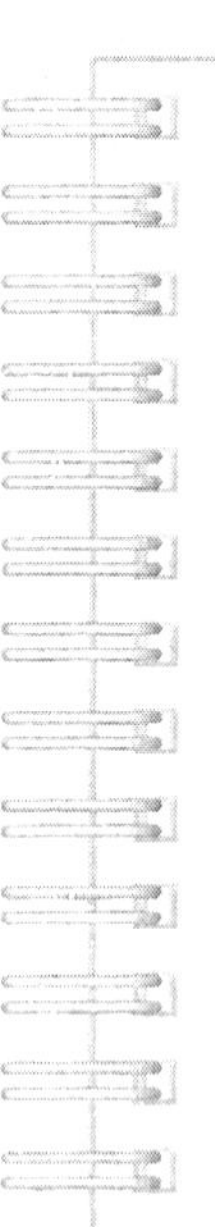

Essential understandings about argument:

1. It is normal to disagree.
2. Disagreement does not always mean one person is right and the other is wrong.
3. It is OK to change your mind when discovering new information or evidence.
4. When people who disagree cooperate, they often come up with the best solutions for everyone.
5. When you listen to the viewpoints of others, you learn and grow.

2. Most students will initially associate the words *argument* and *disagreement* with their experience with friends and family members fighting with each other. Naturally, many of their experiences with argument will be negative. When people are able to calm their emotions, think logically, and share their reasoning with others, they are actually quite likely to work together to make decisions and solve problems in ways that work for everyone involved.

Promoting Strong Persuasive Writing *(cont.)*

3. Use a simple diagram to illustrate the role of uncontrolled emotion versus calm reasoning in argument.

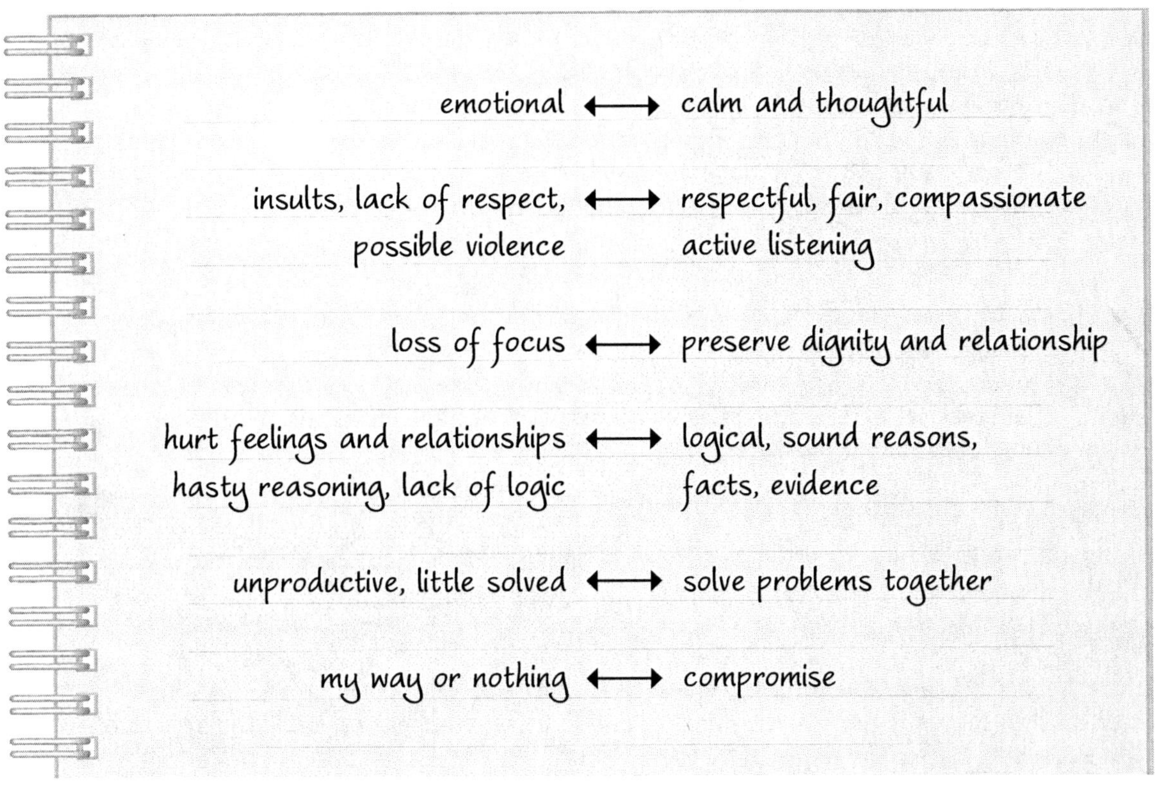

4. Choose an issue that has meaning to the students. For example, students may consider the issue of choosing their own seats in the cafeteria. Have them list reasons why they should have free choice. Then, have them list reasons why adults should assign student seating. Do both sides have good reasons? Does one side seem entirely right while the other is entirely wrong?

5. Just as the truth of an argument is not entirely on one side or the other, students' opinions on an issue may also lie somewhere in the middle. Choose a familiar issue, such as keeping animals in zoos. Have students list as many reasons as they can to show zoos are a good thing and as many reasons as they can that zoos are not good. Then, label one corner of the room *100% Yes to Zoos* and the opposite corner *100% No to Zoos*. Have students position themselves where they stand. Explain that some people may be leaning toward one side or the other. Guide them to stand along the continuum toward the side they favor. Observe how members of a group typically stand at varying positions between two sides of an argument, rather than all the way on one side or the other.

6. Assure students that it is perfectly normal and wise to change one's opinion on an issue when presented with new ideas and information. This is not a sign of weakness—it is evidence of thoughtful reasoning. Use the sentence frames to help students express their shift in thinking: *At first, I thought...* or *But now, I see that...because I learned...*

Promoting Strong Persuasive Writing *(cont.)*

Strategy 7: Writers evaluate the strength of reasoning in persuasive pieces.

EXPLANATION

Strong persuasive pieces present an author's reasoning on a topic. Reasoning is one's logical thinking about an issue in order to draw a conclusion or make a judgment. Reasoning can also mean the reasons and evidence that result from the thinking process. It is easy to think of evaluating the strength of reasoning as too big a topic that is simply too hard for grades 3–5 students, particularly third graders. Reasoning, however, does not have to be a challenging concept for students to master and, in fact, it is a key component of critical thinking. A crux of critical thinking is the ability to evaluate the evidence and the reasons and determine whether the reasoning is solid. An author's reasoning can be faulty, illogical, and not credible, but it can also be solid and strong. Solid reasoning means that one's reason and supporting evidence are logical, relevant, and credible. Strategy 7 focuses on having students slow down, look at the evidence and the reasons, and determine whether the logic is sound. Students will look closely at persuasive messages and evaluate the strength of the reasons and evidence. This is an introductory strategy that paves the way for students to recognize faulty logic as detailed in Strategy 8.

SUPPORT FOR THE STRATEGY

1. Ensure that students have a clear understanding of the terms *reasons* and *evidence* and are able to identify the elements of persuasive writing (see Strategy 3 for how to build students' understanding of the elements of persuasive writing).

2. Define the term *reasoning* for students. Reasoning is *how* and *why* one forms an opinion. In other words, reasoning is the careful thinking one does when trying to make a judgment or draw a conclusion. For example, you need to decide whether to go outside to play or study for your math test. You think about why you may want to play and why you may be better off studying. You consider the fun you will have with your friends, but then you also remember the low grade you got on the last quiz and how your parents might react if you were to get another bad grade. So, you conclude that it is a better idea to study, and you tell your friends you can play tomorrow. This thinking process is called *reasoning*. If someone asks why you are not going to play, you can explain your thinking by saying, "My reasoning is that I want to pass my math test, so I need to study. I got a 65 percent on the last one, and my parents were upset, so I need to spend more time practicing my math problems. I can play tomorrow."

3. Provide examples of reasoning and evidence that support someone's opinion.
    - Emma thinks that we should have zoos because students can learn about different animals, how to care for them, and why we need to protect our wildlife. She says that zoos also protect endangered species. For example, her local zoo has a species of turtle that is completely extinct in the wild.
    - Kerry thinks that students should not have to wear uniforms because schools should encourage student independence and individuality. He does not want the school to tell him what to wear. He polled the other students in the school about uniforms. He found out that 93 percent of students agree that uniforms prevent them from feeling comfortable, and 78 percent felt that uniforms were too expensive and placed an unfair burden on their parents.

Promoting Strong Persuasive Writing *(cont.)*

4. Defining solid or sound reasoning means that the reasons and supporting evidence are logical, relevant, and credible. This also means that the reasons and the evidence presented make sense, are true, and are relevant. Strategy 8 looks closely at the use of faulty logic, so the focus of this strategy is primarily on developing a deep understanding of sound reasoning. This can be a difficult concept (even for adults!), but grades 3–5 students can learn to recognize what makes reasoning sound. Provide students with examples of sound reasoning. Discuss why the reasoning is solid.
    - Gabe thinks that he should be allowed to play *Minecraft* every afternoon because it teaches him important coding and strategy skills.
    - Jackson thinks that bees are the most important insect because they pollinate plants and produce honey.

5. To become strong critical thinkers, students need to know not only what solid reasoning is but also how to evaluate the strength of reasoning. In order to teach students how to evaluate, introduce them to the graphic organizers: Option 1 of the Soundness of Reasons and Evidence (page 113) and Option 2 of the Soundness of Reasons and Evidence (page 114). **Note:** Option 1 is simpler than Option 2, which was designed for students with more background knowledge and strong analytical abilities. Learning how to evaluate the soundness of reasons and evidence is a challenging but manageable critical-thinking skill, even for students in third grade. When initially introducing this type of critical thinking to students, realize they will most likely require teacher support; however, over time, fourth- and fifth-grade students should be able to engage with the texts and graphic organizers more independently. Model how to use a Soundness of Reasons and Evidence graphic organizer. Choose a sample text, such as *Big Food, Big Soda: Ban Supersize Drinks* (page 136). Explain that evaluating the soundness of reasoning means looking for specific clues to tell the reader that the evidence makes sense. For example, if attempting to determine whether the evidence makes sense, highlight clues such as the use of relevant facts and the use of a credible source. Or if attempting to determine whether the author is fair to both sides, look closely at clues to see whether the author is discrediting the other side because he does not like the person or because he does not like the person's argument.

These organizers may present questions to help students think about the strength of a persuasive piece. Teachers may choose to use them to prompt oral discussion or written response.

Promoting Strong Persuasive Writing *(cont.)*

Strategy 8: Writers recognize faulty logic in persuasive pieces.

EXPLANATION

In Strategy 7, students were challenged to become critical thinkers as they analyzed the strength of the reasons and evidence in a piece. If critical thinking is weighing the evidence and making a smart choice, then an important part of being a critical thinker is being able to recognize faulty logic or errors in reasoning in persuasive pieces. Faulty logic is a disconnect between the opinion or claim and the reasons and evidence that the author is using to influence the reader or audience. Often, faulty logic is rooted in a lack of evidence to support the claim. Strategy 8 provides common examples of faulty logic found in persuasive pieces that grades 3–5 students can recognize and understand. Teaching students to identify these faulty elements (sometimes called "logical fallacies") prepares them to think critically and make wise choices when deciding how they will be influenced by the persuasive messages around them.

SUPPORT FOR THE STRATEGY

1. In order for this strategy to make sense to students, they must understand the concept of logic and logical reasoning. Logical arguments are ones that can be proved. They do not appeal to emotions or to the credibility of the author or readers. They are backed up by evidence. Logical reasoning is when the reasoning (opinion, claim, reasons, and evidence) is credible and relevant.
2. Introduce students to the idea of faulty logic. Explain that faulty logic, also known as a logical fallacy, is reasoning when there is a disconnect between the opinion or claim and the reasons and evidence that the author is using to influence the reader or audience. This means that the premise(s) does not equal the conclusion.
3. Introduce students to *TRAPS*: Five Types of Faulty Logic in Persuasive Pieces.

	***TRAPS*: FIVE TYPES OF FAULTY LOGIC IN PERSUASIVE PIECES**
T	**Tradition and popular beliefs**—People say that a hat keeps you from getting sick! So, wear a hat if you do not want a cold!
R	**Refuting a false argument**—Julia claims that sometimes kids need to stand up to bullies. Alexander accuses Julia of being OK with fighting on the playground.
A	**Attacking the character, not the issue**—Do not listen to Nola's ideas for changes to the lunch menu because she is a picky eater.
P	**Phony causes**—Louisa's rescue dog is really nice. He must be happy that he was rescued.
S	**Sweeping generalizations**—My math test last Friday was really hard. I am never going to do well on a math test.

Promoting Strong Persuasive Writing *(cont.)*

4. Share different examples of solid reasoning and faulty logic. Have students determine which is faulty reasoning and which is logical reasoning. If it is an example of faulty logic, have them determine which of the TRAPS it falls under!
   - Nina and Julian were arguing about who knows more about animals. Nina said that Julian knows nothing about animals since he has never been to the zoo.
   - The town councilwoman proposed expanding bus service in the town. She said that public transportation is very important. Research shows that over 70 percent of people in their town take the bus to school or work. Therefore, without public transportation, many people would not be able to get to work or school.
   - Katherine wrote Mia a letter to thank her for being a good friend. She said, "Mia, you are a great friend because you are a good listener and a fun companion."
   - Ida and Ray talked about who they were voting for in the student council election. Ida said that she is voting for Nicholas since he is popular, and popular people make good leaders.
5. Once students have a solid understanding of the elements of faulty logic, have them generate lists of sentences that use solid reasoning and faulty logic. Cut the sentences, and pass them around. Have students read the sentences and sort them into two piles.
6. For further practice, encourage students to look for logical fallacies in the real world. Listen to political speeches; look closely at print and digital advertisements, letters to the editor, and travel brochures or menus; and have fun identifying the common TRAPS that students can find.
7. Have students look through their own writing and find examples of faulty logic or logical fallacies. Encourage them to find creative ways to fix their logic and strengthen their arguments.

Strategy 9: Writers use conversation to develop their ideas.

EXPLANATION

The purpose of this strategy is to move students away from just loudly stating their opinions and to instead learn how to use conversation to develop strong and substantiated views on a topic as a key step in the process of arguing to learn (Andriessen 2006). This strategy encourages students to use group discussions to share opinions and reasoning and to respond to and learn from the thinking of others. Conversation will help students explore and refine their viewpoints as they try out ideas on others and hear what their classmates think. In some cases, they may change their viewpoints based on what they have learned from others! In addition, students who talk through their thinking first are more likely to be able to clearly articulate their ideas in writing later.

SUPPORT FOR THE STRATEGY

1. Like any other skill, the best way to get students to learn to have productive peer-to-peer conversations is to allow them plenty of opportunity to do so. Introduce a turn-and-talk routine, and enact it regularly each day. With regular practice, even students as young as pre-K will turn and talk with purpose and productivity.

Turn and talk:

- Participate in conversations with diverse partners.
- Learn to follow conversational rules.
- Begin to express thoughts, feelings, and ideas with detail.

Things to model and practice:

- a signal to start talking—a bell, a clapping pattern, 1-2-3 sit knee to knee
- turning and sitting—physically turn toward each other and engage in conversation, sitting knee to knee with good posture
- talking—students sharing their answers to a question with their partners, sharing their observations from a read-aloud, brainstorming ideas to plan for drawing and writing, and so on
- conversational rules—looking, listening, staying on topic, and taking turns
- signal to stop and turn back toward the teacher—a bell, a clapping pattern, "3-2-1 talking is done"

Promoting Strong Persuasive Writing *(cont.)*

2. If there are English Learners (ELs) in the class, encourage and support them to use their home language with partners who share their language. Drawing, dictating, and pantomime are effective accommodations, too.
3. Set and model clear guidelines for productive conversation.

4. Emphasize the importance of maintaining respect toward others, even when they disagree with you. See Strategy 6 for more talking points on the benefits of considering multiple viewpoints. Set ground rules, and model good behavior for showing good manners and tolerance even if conversations get passionate. Some conversation prompts to guide students are:
   - Tell me more about why you feel that way.
   - Can you provide evidence to support your thinking?
   - I understand your point, but I disagree because...
5. Use sentence frames to help students speak with clarity and purpose. The chart on page 21 is useful in framing conversation about a variety of genres and topics.

Promoting Strong Persuasive Writing *(cont.)*

Strategy 10: Writers provide logical reasons to back up opinions.

EXPLANATION

It is through relevant and logical reasoning that people are able to persuade critical thinkers to agree or at least lead them to respect their points of view. This strategy not only addresses what it means to provide reasons, but it also addresses what it means to provide *logical* reasons.

SUPPORT FOR THE STRATEGY

1. Tell students that when someone wants to persuade others to agree with his or her opinion, reasons are usually provided for the opinion. Reasons explain *why* people think what they do.
2. Teach related vocabulary, such as *explain, justify, support,* and *back up,* so students can converse about their opinions and reasoning effectively. Use this vocabulary with students in group discussion and one-on-one conferences.
3. Share some examples of your own opinions and reasons. Have the students ask why.
4. Teach students to use webbing or a graphic organizer to plan opinions and reasons.

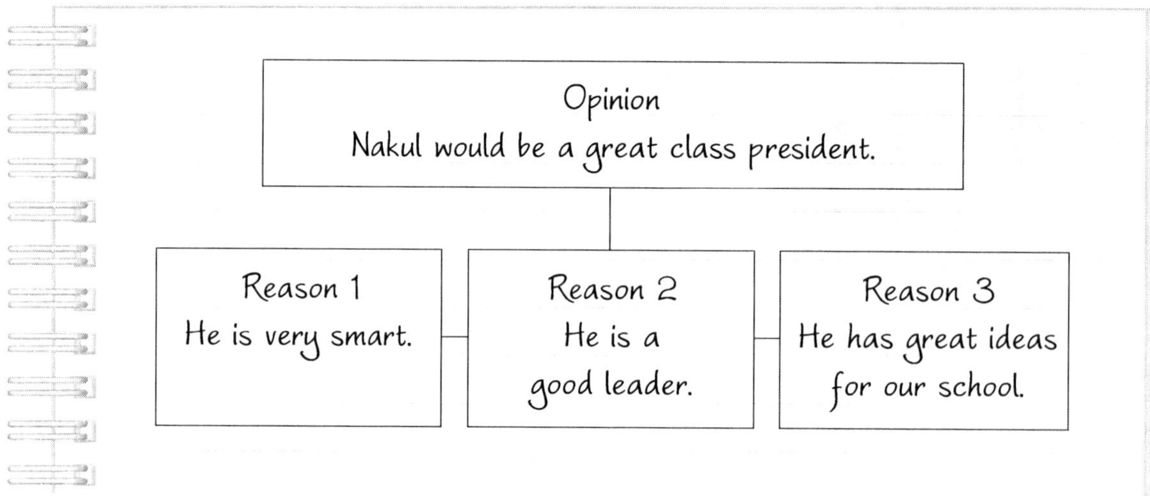

5. Post a large sign where students can see it. The sign should simply say, "I think so because..." When someone expresses an opinion, prompt him or her to follow up with one or more reasons using this sentence starter.
6. Play hand games to reinforce the opinion and reasons concept. Play using simple opinions, but also try out opinions on slightly more complex issues such as *There should be no homework on weekends* or *Everyone should play sports.*
7. Once students' understanding of reasons is solid, move on to the concept of *logical* reasoning. A logical reason is a reason based on thoughtful consideration of evidence and the relationships between relevant factors in order to reach a conclusion.

Forming Logical Reasons

- Gather as much information (facts, explanations, statistics, expert opinions, etc.) as you can about your subject from reliable sources.
- Learn from others. Be ready to learn new things and maybe change your mind. You may develop a new opinion, new reasons, or both.
- Once you have done your research, use what you learned to make a claim and use logical reasoning to back it.
- Base your reasons on information not emotion.
- Question your reasoning. Does it make sense? Is it true?

8. Help students learn *how to* develop logical reasons by thinking deeply about the topic, considering the available information, and possibly seeking out more to build a foundation of reasons and conclusions. The first reasons that come to mind are not always the most logical ones. Impulsive reasoning is often based on emotion and assumptions. Let's say a child tries to convince his parent to get him a parrot. The parent, after saying no about 100 times, finally asks, "Why in the world would you want a parrot for a pet?!?" The child responds, "It would be fun! A parrot would make a great pet! They are smart. They are easy to care for." The parent replies, "Those are reasons, but I am not sure you have thought this through." As it turns out, the parent is right. The child did not supply these reasons based on logic, and the parent is wise not to be convinced by his hasty reasoning. The parent may ask questions such as, "Why would it be fun to have a parrot? Do you know anyone who has a parrot? What is so great about parrots? What might not be great? How do you know they are smart? Are they easy to care for? How long do they live? How much does it cost to keep a parrot?" At this point, the child may back down, or he may double down and do some research to provide reasons based on logic.

9. Use this series of questions to evaluate the logic of a reason. The child in the parrot example may have passed the first three items, but not necessarily the fourth or fifth.
    - Is the reason stated clearly?
    - Is the reason related to the opinion/claim?
    - Does the reason attempt to explain why the opinion/claim is sound?
    - Is the reason supported by evidence? (personal experience or research)
    - Do the conclusions make sense?

Promoting Strong Persuasive Writing *(cont.)*

Strategy 11: Writers provide evidence to support reasons.

EXPLANATION

As stated in Strategy 10, a *reason* is a cause, an explanation, or a justification for an event, an action, an opinion, or a claim. For example, if a writer claims that there should be a law against smoking, he or she may provide the reason that smoking is bad for people's health. This reason would justify the author's claim that such a law is necessary. This reason by itself, however, is much more persuasive when supported by evidence. *Evidence* provides information to support the reason, or proof. For example, "Cigarette smoking causes 443,000 deaths per year." This statistic provides proof that smoking is bad for one's health, making the reason and the overall claim more logical and convincing. This strategy supports students in understanding what evidence is, the rationale for providing it, and various types of evidence that will strengthen the reasoning in their persuasive writing.

SUPPORT FOR THE STRATEGY

1. Build a strong foundational understanding of a reason. See Strategy 7.
2. Define *evidence* for students, and discuss its relationship to opinions and reasons. Evidence is information that verifies the truth of something, or proof. Evidence backs up a reason. A writer may say people should avoid eating bacon because it is unhealthy. The bacon lovers of the world may reject this reason without some evidence to back it up. For example, "Bacon contains nitrites, which have been proven to cause cancer." (But as we well know, even with evidence, bacon lovers still may not care!) There is no question, however, that evidence strengthens reasoning. The reasons that are rooted in evidence are considered logical and more convincing than reasons that are not. Evidence helps a writer prove that her reasons for her opinion are true.
3. Provide examples, such as the Opinion + Reason + Evidence chart, illustrated below.

Opinion
Everyone should stop smoking.

+

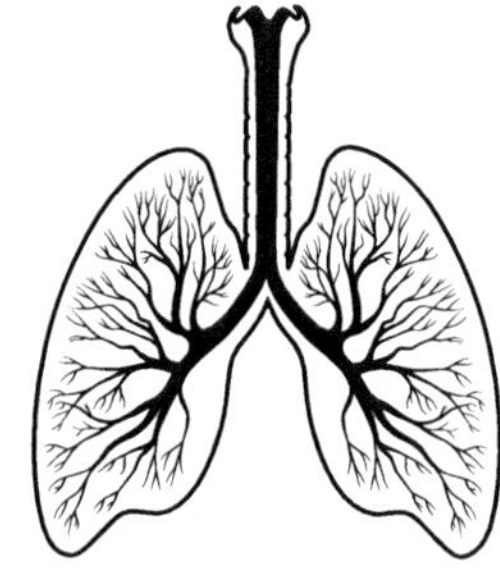

Reason
Smoking is bad for people's health.

+

Evidence
According to the American Lung Association, 443,000 people die from smoking or secondhand smoke every year. This is almost three times more than alcohol, AIDS, car accidents, drug use, murder, and suicide combined.

Promoting Strong Persuasive Writing *(cont.)*

4. Evidence may come in many forms, including these common types. Define and discuss them with students.
   - facts and statistics (best if the source is provided)
   - examples
   - anecdotes (e.g., a story that backs up a point)
   - sensory details, description (see, hear, smell, taste, feel)
   - expert opinion or testimonials
   - quotations from credible texts/sources
5. Read persuasive texts with your students in search of evidence. Look for the types listed here. Add to the list if you find other types of evidence. Be sure to explore genres that may not have much evidence, such as advertisements and visual texts.
6. Encourage students to research to find evidence—original and from outside sources. Original research is research you have conducted yourself, such as interviews, experiments, surveys, or personal experience and anecdotes. Students should also search for evidence from various texts that has been supplied and compiled by others, such as books, periodicals, and websites. See Strategy 12 for more information.
7. Regardless of what variety of sources you use, they must be credible. In other words, your sources must be reliable, accurate, and trustworthy.

Promoting Strong Persuasive Writing *(cont.)*

Strategy 12: Writers use research to support their opinions.

EXPLANATION

In this strategy, students gather information and facts to support their opinion through both primary and secondary research. They are old enough to understand what plagiarism is and develop ethical habits when it comes to using other people's work. Teachers should also encourage students to conduct primary research when possible, especially when they are writing about topics that affect their families, schools, and local communities. Primary research is information that the students gather directly themselves using methods such as interviews, surveys and polls, direct observations, collection of artifacts, and photographic evidence.

SUPPORT FOR THE STRATEGY

1. Reiterate that in order to support our opinions and reasoning, it is very persuasive when we can also use facts to back up our ideas. Provide students with access to informational text via books, magazines, and the Internet to learn about topics that interest them, develop opinions and reasoning, and find evidence that supports their thinking. See Our Favorite Informational Websites on pages 32–34: Our Informational Favorite Magazines on page 66. Third graders are ready to learn to take notes when gathering information from informational sources. Teachers may find that this age group benefits from going old-school when learning to take notes. You will need note cards and rubber bands to keep notes together. Provide students with note cards. Have them record one fact per note card. One benefit of doing this is that they can later sort their note cards to match their reasons, helping to ensure that they line up their reasons with relevant facts.

2. This is a great age to build a habit of paraphrasing the work of others and break students' tendency to copy directly from sources. See the image below for a simple strategy that works.

***NOTETAKING*: IN YOUR WORDS**	
STOP	when you find good information for your piece.
COVER	up the text.
THINK	about what the text said.
PARAPHRASE	the information in writing in your own words.
TIPS	▫ Use same meaning but different words. ▫ Use synonyms. ▫ Change sentence order.

SECTION 4

Promoting Strong Persuasive Writing *(cont.)*

3. Introduce students to the concept of source credibility. Credible sources are those the reader can trust to provide accurate information. Students must begin to understand not to believe everyone and everything out there, especially online. Do not be shy to actively guide them in finding credible sources and avoiding shaky ones. If you choose to provide students with a menu of credible sources, be sure to take the time to explain how you evaluated them as a teachable moment. Here are some guidelines you may use and share with students:

Characteristics of Credible Sources

- The author is named and is an expert on the subject.
- The source is produced by an organization that has expertise on the subject and is up to date.
- The main purpose of the source is to inform, not to sell anything.
- The author uses correct spelling and grammar. Formatting is professional looking.
- The language is respectful and appropriate.
- If online, the site is *not* full of "tricking you to click" advertisements.
- The source is a published informational book or encyclopedia.
- The source is a mainstream magazine or newspaper.
- The information in the source matches other credible sources.

4. Explain that while information in books, magazines, and websites can be very useful, people also have the power to gather information themselves—interviewing people with knowledge about the topic, conducting polls and surveys, taking photographs, gathering artifacts, or direct observation.

5. Students can interview experts on their topics to learn new and interesting facts. Experts can be classmates, teachers, or family members who have depth of knowledge on a topic. Prior to their interview, have students write 6–10 interview questions about the topic that they would like to ask their interviewee.

SECTION 4

Promoting Strong Persuasive Writing *(cont.)*

Tech Support for the Strategy

- Students use an online polling/surveying tool such as SurveyMonkey or Kahoot.
- Students use a graphic tool like the one found at nces.ed.gov/nceskids/.
- Students use digital resources, including informational websites (see list of websites on pages 32–33) and informational videos, to compile their research.
- Students record their research on a note-taking site such as Evernote.com, Google Doc, Word, or Pages.
- Help students create bibliographies with ease using online tools such as easybib.com or citationmachine.net.

OUR FAVORITE INFORMATIONAL MAGAZINES

Check out these publications for various examples of persuasive pieces.

MAGAZINE	CONTENT
Ask Magazine	There are numerous articles and features address topics related to art, science, inventors, and more.
Click Magazine	Read articles and features that address topics related to art, science, nature, the environment, and more.
National Geographic Kids	Find articles and features that address topics related to animals, interesting places, and more.
Ranger Rick	Many articles and features are available to address topics related to animals, science, nature, and more.
Scholastic DynaMath	Read articles and features that address student-friendly topics of interest with math connections.
Scholastic Flix	Separate series offer texts and features that address science, history, and fiction-nonfiction sets.
Scholastic News	There are articles and features that address topics related to current events and other areas of interest.
Time for Kids	Find articles and features that address topics related to current events and other areas of interest.

Promoting Strong Persuasive Writing *(cont.)*

Strategy 13: Writers match evidence to the audience, purpose, and reasoning.

EXPLANATION

This strategy suggests that students should think critically about the type of evidence they gather and focus their efforts to best match the audience, purpose, and reasoning of their piece. Teachers guide students through thinking about what specific kinds of evidence they need and planning how to collect it. This is a great time to tap into the suggestions for Strategy 12 by encouraging students to not only do traditional research using secondary sources but to also gather primary sources and even do original research via methods such as interviews, polls, and photography.

SUPPORT FOR THE STRATEGY

1. Students will need a basic understanding of the concepts mentioned in the strategy: evidence, audience, purpose, and reasoning.
    - **Evidence:** information that backs up the what the writer is trying to say
      Our school library only has 1,000 books in it. That is not even two per student!
    - **Audience:** someone the writer hopes will read the piece and make a difference
      the principal who may buy more books for the library
    - **Purpose:** the reason for writing the piece
      to persuade the school to buy more books for the library
    - **Reasoning:** how and why someone develops an opinion or a claim
      the reasons and evidence that the writer provides to support his or her opinion
2. Review the types of evidence that a writer may gather in general. For example:
    - facts and statistics (best if the source is provided)
    - examples
    - anecdotes (e.g., a story that backs a point)
    - sensory details and description (see, hear, smell, taste, feel)
    - expert opinion or testimonials
    - quotations from credible texts/sources
3. Model how to think about matching evidence to audience, purpose, and reasoning.

    Audience: Let me think. Who is my audience? What am I trying to get them to do? What type of information may be important to them or get their attention? For example, if I were writing a persuasive letter to my parents about getting a new puppy, I want to think like my parents do. I know they would be worried that I will not take care of the puppy. Maybe I could think of some specific examples of when I showed responsibility. I also know they worry about the cost. Maybe I could find a fact about the cost of owning a dog in New York City and find a shelter near my home.

SECTION 4

Promoting Strong Persuasive Writing *(cont.)*

Purpose: My purpose is the main goal of my piece. If my goal is to get people to rescue dogs from animal shelters, maybe I could find evidence of how many dogs need homes in our country. I could also try to find a fact about how many dogs may die if no one rescues them. I could even include a picture of a sad-looking dog to show how a dog might feel being stuck in a shelter. Maybe I could interview someone who rescued a dog and have them tell me how it made their life better.

Reasoning: I want to make sure that I provide evidence that supports the reasons for my opinion. If I am writing a piece with the main opinion that it is important to eat a healthy breakfast, one of my reasons could be that eating breakfast helps kids concentrate at school. Maybe I could tell about a time I forgot to eat breakfast and how I felt sleepy and out of focus at school. Or maybe I could find a study that says that kids who eat breakfast do better in school.

4. Have students practice with hypothetical examples or with their own writing topics. Ask them what types of evidence they would gather for:
    - an opinion piece on the best kind of playground equipment for the school to purchase
    - an opinion piece on whether students should have homework
    - an opinion piece that persuades other students to recycle
    - an opinion piece on the best class pet
    - an opinion piece that declares Mrs. Chamberlin the best teacher ever

Promoting Strong Persuasive Writing *(cont.)*

Strategy 14: Writers use effective words and phrases to connect ideas.

EXPLANATION

In this strategy, students are asked to think about how authors use language to help readers follow the flow of their thinking. Authors use linking words and phrases to help keep their writing smooth and easy to read by sending important signals that more related information is coming. Linking words and phrases, such as *for example* and *furthermore*, can be used to connect ideas, reasons, or even sections. (*Furthermore, Nakul would make a great class president because he is kind to everyone.*) This is an essential academic-language skill.

By separating the opinion statement from the supporting reason, the writer is able to broaden the scope of why Nakul would make a great class president. The accompanying lesson in Section 5 demonstrates how to separate the opinion statement from the reasons and provides students with an opportunity to practice this skill.

SUPPORT FOR THE STRATEGY

1. Gradually, teach students commonly used linking words and phrases, such as those on page 119. Use them frequently in writing. Keep a chart posted near where you conduct shared writing and modeling. Use another marker or font to emphasize where you use these words.
2. Practice using the words orally. Make a dramatic show when you use them.
3. As powerful as explicit practice is, one of the best ways for students to absorb academic language in general is by hearing it in use. Reading aloud from magazine and newspaper articles and other informational texts written for students will ground students in academic language and increase the chances they will know how to use such words when they need them. Provide students with a persuasive piece (see Section 6), and have them underline or circle examples of linking words and phrases. Have them choose their favorites and use them to compose sentences, one with a stand-alone opinion and the following one with a linking word or phrase that connects the reason to the opinion.
4. *For example* is a power phrase in the academic language world. Teach students the power of using it to provide explanation and clarity to their ideas. Use prompts to practice. Present a prompt, then have students provide an example using *For example*.
   - Our class reads a lot of good books.
   - Our school offers many fun activities each year.
   - Our town has many interesting places to visit.
   - There are a lot of ways we can protect our environment.
   - There are many reasons not to smoke.
   - Our principal does many nice things for the students in our school.
   - There are many ways kids our age can demonstrate kindness to others.
5. Linking words are a powerful tool for students as they learn how to provide solid evidence, refute the counterargument, and develop their persuasive messages. One way to have students strengthen their writing is to encourage them to revise their persuasive pieces linking words and phrases. They can add in linking words to connect ideas, cite sources, add additional evidence, and much more (see Strategy 19).

Promoting Strong Persuasive Writing *(cont.)*

Strategy 15: Writers establish a credible, persuasive voice and tone.

EXPLANATION

Persuasive voice and tone refers to the enthusiasm, personality, and spirit of the writer as it comes through the words on the page or oral presentation of a piece, or both. Writing with little persuasive voice may seem flat, distant, and quite often less convincing than writing with strong persuasive voice. Strong voice can convey contagious passion for the topic and may sometimes even be convincing despite evidence that is not especially strong. Of course, a balance of passion with credible knowledge is an especially powerful combination. In persuasive writing, an awareness of audience is important. In most cases, a piece should project an appropriate tone that is relatively serious and polite and avoids excessive humor or rudeness. Appropriate control of voice and tone is linked closely to credibility with the audience. A writer must consider what kind of personality would best appeal to the targeted audience of a piece. Strategy 15 helps students become aware of these elements and adjust their writing in effective ways.

SUPPORT FOR THE STRATEGY

1. Use the content of the explanation paragraph above as support when explaining persuasive voice and tone to students.
2. Look for pieces that convey a strong persuasive voice to use as read-alouds. See Section 6 for some resources. Some characteristics:
    - The writer seems passionate and knowledgeable about his or her topic and purpose.
    - The writer appears aware of the audience and the desire to persuade them.
    - The writing is engaging and maintains energy and enthusiasm throughout the piece.
    - The writer may address the audience directly—using second-person pronouns, such as *you* and *your*.
    - The writer shows respect toward opposing points of view.
    - The writer uses a tone that matches purpose, audience, and topic. For example, in a piece about a somber topic, the writer maintains a serious tone. Or in a piece written for a person in a position of authority, the writer consistently uses a respectful tone.
    - The writer uses carefully chosen words to emphasize the point. For example, the writer uses adjectives and verbs that evoke strong images and emotions.
    - The writer lets his or her personality and voice shine through the use of punctuation and font.
    - The writer uses specific names that make the author and story seem more real (*Joey's Diner* versus *a restaurant*, *The Sooper Looper* versus *an amusement park ride*).
    - The writer uses quotes or dialogue.
    - The writer uses conversational language.
3. Read a persuasive piece aloud with and without passion to demonstrate the impact of expression in oral presentation.
4. Read sample persuasive pieces with the class, and ask students to evaluate the writer's success in conveying a persuasive voice and tone.
5. When students successfully convey persuasive voice, read their work aloud to the class as exemplars, and articulate what they did well.

Promoting Strong Persuasive Writing *(cont.)*

Strategy 16: Writers add visual support to express and clarify ideas.

EXPLANATION

So many of the persuasive messages we see daily depend heavily on visuals. A rescue-dog organization may have a poster of a sad puppy to tug at our heartstrings and encourage us to adopt a dog. An advertisement for a cereal may show a happy and healthy-looking child eating the cereal. Everywhere we look, persuasive messages are strengthened by images. We encourage students to examine the visuals that accompany persuasive messages and once again think about author choice. How do the details in the image go along with what the author is saying?

When students write about their opinions, we ask them to think about what visuals they can provide to support their ideas. Can they include a picture that gives more information about the topic or touch the reader's emotions? Are there facts they can show with a simple chart, graph, or diagram? Hand-drawn illustrations are perfectly appropriate and effective for grades 3–5 writing, but we should also encourage students to use photographs or other digital sources for images, if possible.

In the lesson that accompanies this strategy, we have students look over one of their persuasive pieces and add visual support to strengthen their message.

SUPPORT FOR THE STRATEGY

1. Share the *Big Food, Big Soda: Ban Supersize Drinks* (page 36). Discuss *how* images would strengthen the message.
2. Conduct close readings of persuasive messages with visual support. We provide many suggestions of where to find such texts in Section 3 of this book. Ask, "How do the details in the image go along with what the author is saying? How does the image persuade you to believe the writer's views?"
3. Open students' eyes to the many ways they can provide images—by drawing, from photographs (cell phones are great), and digital images found online. In addition, simple charts, graphs, and diagrams may help them provide important information to their writing.
4. When students create visuals to support their own writing, guide them to add details to their visuals that strengthen their message.

SECTION 4

Tech Support for This Strategy

- Use an app like Popplet to create a visual of a persuasive message.
- Use PowerPoint or Keynote to create a presentation that mixes words and images.
- Compile a collection of visuals for students to use from Google Images or informational websites that have information on the topic.

Promoting Strong Persuasive Writing *(cont.)*

5. Four quick ways to add details to drawings:
   - Add details to the main character or object in the drawing.
   - Add details to show the main character or object in action.
   - Add details to the background setting.
   - Add talk or thought bubbles.
6. Encourage students to use emotion to add details to the characters in their drawing to strengthen their message. It is simple to teach students how to do this, even if the teacher is not artistically inclined. See below for an illustration that illustrates how slight changes in facial details can clearly signal a character's feelings.

SECTION 4

Promoting Strong Persuasive Writing *(cont.)*

Strategy 17: Writers write structured opinion pieces.

EXPLANATION

The goal of this strategy is to introduce students to writing structured pieces that include the elements of a strong opinion piece. These elements should include (at minimum) a clearly stated opinion, one or more reasons to support the opinion, and a concluding section or sentence. Most students are ready to write multiparagraph pieces with an opening section that introduces the main opinion or claim, body paragraphs that supply reasons and evidence, and a conclusion that sums up the piece. We recommend that you use the tools from earlier strategies to guide students' thinking.

SUPPORT FOR THE STRATEGY

1. To ensure that students have a complete understanding of a well-written opinion piece, introduce and explain each of the components:
   - a title
   - an introductory or opening section with an engaging lead that introduces the main opinion or claim
   - body paragraphs that supply reasons and evidence to support the opinion or claim and group ideas logically
   - a conclusion or a concluding section that sums up the piece and often a call-to-action statement
2. Read aloud from an enlarged version of an opinion piece such as *Buses Should Have Seat Belts* (page 138), and model how to identify each segment of the opinion piece. Model how to annotate the piece. Keep it visible for students as they work to compose their own persuasive messages to use as a reference and support.
3. Consider comparing two pieces so students understand that there are many ways to craft an introduction. Discuss how introductions have two important roles. First, they introduce the topic and state the opinion or claim, and second, they should have an engaging lead that makes a reader want to read the whole piece!
4. Then, look at the introductory sentence of *Zoos: Good for Animals and People* (page 135), and discuss how this introductory section differs. What is different about how the author introduces the topic? Look at each element, and notice what is different and what is similar. Discuss different ways to compose an introductory section, such as starting with an opinion statement or starting with a question.

   Begin with the opinion statement: *Skateboarding is the best sport.*

   Begin with a statement about the topic: *I read "From the Mixed-up Files of Mrs. Basil E. Frankweiler" by E.L. Konigsburg. It was great!*

   Begin with a description of a problem: *Sometimes, kids are mean to others on the playground.*

   Begin with a question: *When you finish a soda, do you take the time to recycle the can or bottle?*

Promoting Strong Persuasive Writing *(cont.)*

Begin with a "sound word" (onomatopoeia): *Swish! That's the sound it makes when I make a basket in the greatest game ever!*

Begin with a short story: *The other day, I was walking on the beach. I saw a lot of garbage on the sand. This made me sad.*

Begin by addressing the reader: *Do you think sharks are scary?*

Begin with an exclamation: *Help! Fire!*

5. Writers in grades 3–5 are ready to develop more effective conclusions or concluding statements. They may still prefer to write *The End* in tiny letters at the bottom of the page, but with some clear guidance and fun tips, students can learn the art of crafting effective conclusions. Here are some easy and effective ways to close a piece that students can try:

   End with a strong emotion: *Volunteering in my community garden has changed my life.*

   End with a superlative: *Harry Potter is the best book character!*

   End with a universal word: *Everyone should write thank-you notes.*

   End with a bold statement on the topic: *We need more field trips now!*

   End with a command or a call-to-action statement: *Stop littering today!*

6. When students are ready to provide multiple reasons for their opinions, we recommend providing them with a graphic organizer to plan their ideas.
   a. Brainstorm a list of possible topics (see Section 2 for ideas).
   b. Model how to choose an opinion or a claim on a topic to highlight in a piece of persuasive writing. Provide students with time to select their own topics and determine their opinion on the topic.
   c. Introduce the *Persuasive Writing Planner* graphic organizer on page 120. Model how to add information to it. Consider using tools from Strategies 9 and 11 when modeling how to gather supporting evidence.
   d. Provide students with time to complete their own Persuasive Writing Planner graphic organizers.

Promoting Strong Persuasive Writing *(cont.)*

Strategy 18: Writers express opinions in a variety of genres.

EXPLANATION

Writing in a variety of persuasive writing forms allows students practice in writing for different purposes and for different audiences. Each form of persuasive writing requires a range of skills and emphasizes different strategies. We recommend providing students with the chance to practice writing in a variety of genres. See our list of Traditional and Innovative Forms of Persuasive Writing in Section 3 (page 35). Reaching beyond the opinion paragraph not only addresses a variety of learning styles, but it also helps ensure that students experience the kinds of persuasive writing that they are likely to encounter in the world around them.

SUPPORT FOR THE STRATEGY

1. There are so many great traditional and innovative genres that our students can experiment with. Use the genre table for suggestions on how to approach some of the more unusual genres so that students can try writing in them.

GENRE	WHAT STUDENT WRITERS MIGHT DO...
Advertisements	◆ Compose a simple script for a TV or radio commercial and perform it. ◆ Write a jingle for a product. ◆ Write a slogan for a product or a destination. ◆ Design an advertisement poster, adding text and illustrations. ◆ Design a newspaper or magazine-style ad, adding text and illustrations. ◆ Design a billboard for a product. ◆ Design a promotional T-shirt.
Bumper sticker	◆ Exercise smart word choice to create a slogan for a bumper sticker. ◆ Use bumper stickers to present a call-to-action statement on an issue, an advertisement, or a campaign promotion.
Debates	An age-appropriate procedure: ◆ Students split into two teams that have different stances on an issue. ◆ Each team plans a clear statement of opinion and several reasons to back up their thinking. ◆ Each team takes turns presenting their ideas. ◆ They then have a chance to ask each other questions and respond to each other.
Greeting card	◆ Students create greeting cards that express loving opinions. ◆ Inside the card, they list reasons to back up their opinions.

SECTION 4

Promoting Strong Persuasive Writing *(cont.)*

Infographics	◆ Students choose a topic and study the facts/statistics. ◆ They form opinions about it. ◆ They choose facts/statistics, create simple charts/diagrams, and gather images. ◆ They arrange the information and visuals in a clear, visually engaging way.
Job application (classroom job application)	◆ Teachers posts a variety of classroom jobs that are available. ◆ Students write letters or fill out teacher-created applications to their teacher for class jobs. ◆ They provide opinions about and reasons that they are qualified for the job.
Pantomime	◆ Students play charades, using movements without words to express an opinion about a topic. ◆ Other students will guess the topic, the opinion, and any reasons the actor conveys.
Persuasive slide show presentation (PowerPoint, KeyNote, Prezi)	Students create slide shows on topics that include: ◆ one slide that presents a clear opinion. ◆ additional slides that present reasons to back up the opinion. ◆ illustrations or photos to add more information to each slide.
Playacting	◆ Students plan and act out a short scene related to an opinion statement or a claim. No written script is required. The audience may be challenged to guess what the lesson is. ◆ Students create short skits to rehearse and perform for the class.
Poetry	◆ Write list poems, with opinion stems, such as "My brother is awesome because..." or "Happiness is..." ◆ Create shape poems in the shapes of their favorite options. ◆ Create opinion acrostic poems on the topics they spell out.
Travel brochures	◆ Create brochures that promote fun things about their school. ◆ Create brochures that invite people to visit favorite places around town. ◆ Create brochures for favorite family destinations. ◆ Create brochures for the country his or her family comes from.

2. Conduct a multigenre project. Students choose a topic and create two or more pieces in different genres.

    - A student writes an opinion essay on Philadelphia being a great place to visit. She also creates a travel brochure and a bumper sticker.
    - A student believes that he should be elected class president. He writes a campaign speech, a persuasive letter to the school newspaper, and creates a slogan for the morning announcements.
    - A student makes a claim that the town should have a skating rink. She writes a letter to the mayor. She also creates a poster with a slogan and a detailed illustration and/or a PowerPoint with reasons why the town should act on this idea.

Promoting Strong Persuasive Writing *(cont.)*

Strategy 19: Writers revise for publication.

EXPLANATION

Revision is a crucial part of the writing process. Revision is different from editing, which focuses on language rules and conventions (see Strategy 20). While students may have learned what it means to revise, they are often not given sufficient scaffolding and explicit instructions in the revision process. Often, the revision and editing processes are combined, and work as a brief add-on to the project before hastily beginning a new writing piece. It is very important to provide students with a clear task and specific items to look for. Strategies 19, 20, and 21 are the strategies that let students finalize their persuasive pieces, feel confident about their work, and empower them to use their voices to share their informed views.

SUPPORT FOR THE STRATEGY

1. Before expecting students to revise, define what revision is, explain why writers revise, and model the revision process for them. Model a specific way to revise in a piece of your own writing (see step 2), and then ask students to try it that way on their own writing.

***revision* = *re* + *vision* means "to see again"**

- The purpose of revision is to allow the writer to rework the writing so that it better matches the original goals of the piece.
- Additions or deletions are made by the writer to clarify meaning and strengthen the power of the writing.

***Editing* derives from the Latin word *editus*, meaning "brought forth or produced."**

- The purpose of editing is to make a written piece ready to be presented to a reader.
- This involves making corrections in *conventions*—punctuation, capitalization, spelling, and grammar—to make the writing easier to read.

2. Some ways grades 3–5 students can revise are provided:
    - adding words or sentences to clarify or enhance the meaning of the piece
    - adding visuals or multimedia to enhance and clarify the message
    - deleting a sentence or changing a part that does not make sense
    - adding an attention-grabbing opener
    - adding a clearly stated opinion that states a point of view
    - adding a logical reason to support the opinion

Promoting Strong Persuasive Writing *(cont.)*

- adding evidence to support the reason
- checking that the evidence matches the intended audience, purpose, and reasoning
- adding explanations that clarify the thinking about the opinion
- adding a call-to-action statement
- adding effective words and phrases to connect ideas
- adding at least one persuasive writing technique (ethos, pathos, logos)
- checking for proper citation of sources

3. Only expect students to effectively revise for writing elements that you have specifically taught. It is most effective to ask students to revise for one or two specific things rather than open revision, which can be overwhelming.

4. At this grade level, a simple acronym, COPS Editing, can help students (and teachers!) remember the key editing components. COPS stands for capitalization, order and usage of sentences, punctuation, and spelling. See the sample Persuasive Writing COPS Editing Checklist on page 116. Model practical ways that students can physically make revisions.

5. Have students read their pieces out loud when revising. This increases the odds that they will find errors of omission or sentences that do not make sense.

6. Some students do their best revisions in conference with a teacher. Start the teacher-led portion of the conference by giving at least two compliments on things the student did well. Consider placing stickers on their papers where they did something well.

7. Peer revision is a great way of supporting students as they learn to revise their own writing. At this level, peer revision works best when there is a specific focus. The role of the peer assistant is to compliment the author on things he or she did well and possibly to collaborate

When we revise and edit together, we:

- decide whose writing we will focus on first.
- name specific items we will be revising for meaning, tone, and argument technique.
- determine how we will indicate textual evidence of each item on the checklist.
- are kind and supportive.
- find things we like in one another's work and offer helpful suggestions.

on one or two focused developmentally appropriate ways to revise, for example, using strong verbs or listening for sentences that do not make sense.

8. Provide students with questions to ask each other: "How did I do on using descriptive words?", "How did I do with adding an example of ethos to my writing?", or "How did I do on the ending?" Use the Persuasive Writing COPS Editing Checklist in Section 6, page 116, and customize it according to what has been taught. It is recommended to begin using this type of checklist in a conference between a teacher and a student and to then gradually help students build independence so they can use it on their own.

9. Many students do not do well with working with a traditional revision checklists on their own. Some students may use them effectively, but others will simply check the boxes regardless of what they wrote or just "forget" to use the list. A better tool for these writers is an active checklist. An active checklist prompts students to actively mark the location of required elements in their pieces. This tends to make students more accountable by turning their attention directly on their writing and the good things they included. A teacher may guide a group of students through this checklist by reading it aloud to them. Some prompts that may appear on an active checklist:
    - Underline your opinion statement in green.
    - Draw a **smiley face** next to your best reason.
    - Write an **E** next to your favorite piece of evidence.
    - Is something missing from your piece? Now is the time to add it.

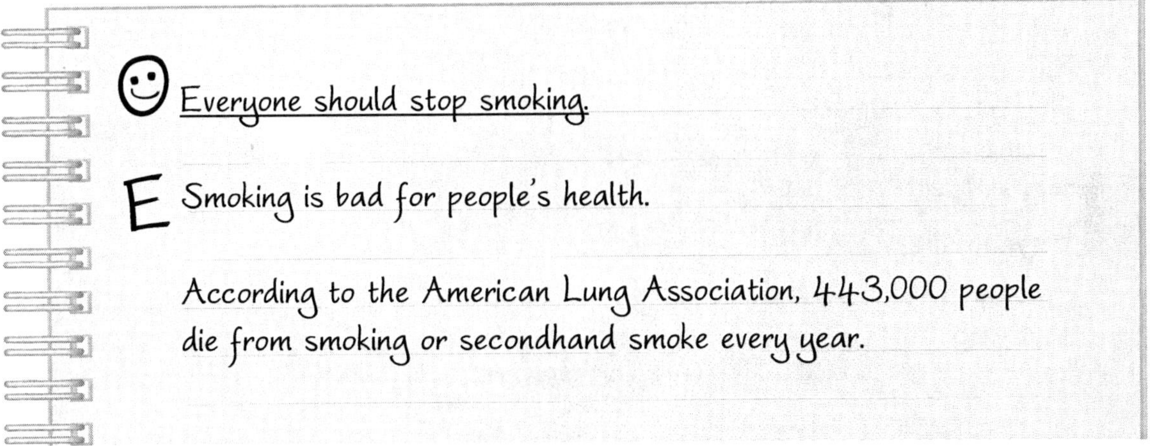

10. Targeted revision can be very effective after a writing lesson. Here is how this may look:
    - A teacher teaches a lesson on using effective words and phrases to connect ideas. The students then go back to already written pieces in their writing folders and practice adding effective words and phrases to connect their ideas.
    - A teacher teaches a lesson on adding a reason to support the opinion to a piece. The students then go back to the drafts they are working on and find a good place to add a reason to support the opinion.
    - A teacher teaches a lesson on writing conclusions and models three techniques to end a persuasive piece. The students choose already written pieces and write three possible endings. They choose the best one and add it to their pieces.

SECTION 4

Promoting Strong Persuasive Writing *(cont.)*

Strategy 20: Writers edit for publication.

EXPLANATION

Editing is the process of proofreading a piece for errors in conventions, or the rules and patterns of the English language. Conventions include elements such as punctuation, capitalization, sentence structure, tense and agreement, and spelling. Teachers should teach conventions skills explicitly through modeling and practice, and gently encourage students to apply as much as they can every time they write. Some writers lack confidence in their skills or get bogged down with their desire for conventional perfection. They may continually ask how to spell words or keep their writing very simple to avoid errors. We reassure these students that it is OK to take risks and get their ideas down on paper, as they will have the opportunity to make corrections during the editing stage.

SUPPORT FOR THE STRATEGY

1. To teach conventions, choose a skill—*using correct capitalization*, for example. Teach and reinforce the skill in a variety of ways:
   - Name and notice the use of the skill during shared-reading experiences. "Let's notice how this author capitalizes the name of people and places..."
   - Model applying the strategy in writing during shared-writing experiences. "Watch me write a paragraph. Notice how I capitalize the name of people and places in each appropriate sentence..."
   - Guide students to apply the skill in writing as part of a dictation. "Write this sentence down as I say it. Do not forget to capitalize the names of people and places."
   - Guide students to apply the skill in their own independent writing. "Today, when you write, I want you to remember to capitalize any names of people and places you use."
   - Reinforce the skill in writing conferences. "Let's check how you did with capitalizing the names of people and places."
2. Use the following tips to help guide students to edit effectively.
3. Help students understand that the purpose of conventions is to make our writing easier for others to read. Use language such as, "Your reader may get confused if you used a period instead of a question mark" to reinforce that concept.
4. Do not expect students to get it all right when they write. Students should be able to take some risks with conventions they do not yet understand. That said, it is OK to gently require that students apply skills you have already taught by doing their best to get it right the first time. Be explicit: "When you write today, be sure that you're using quotation marks to show direct quotes from the text." Then, work the room to praise students who remembered. The consequence for forgetting is a gentle reminder for those who forgot.

Tips for Effective Editing

- Leave time between drafting and editing for the brain to reset and see the piece with fresh eyes. Consider doing a quick edit at the start of every writing period as opposed to the more commonly assigned end of the period.
- Encourage students, even those working alone, to read their piece aloud. The brain tends to hear more errors that way.
- Some students will hear more order and usage errors when listening to their writing read by another student or the teacher.
- To check spelling, read the text backward, one word at a time. Removing context helps errors stand out.
- Reading with exaggerated expression helps emphasize where punctuation is needed (pauses, questions, exclamation points, etc.).
- Provide a short list to students with extensive errors. This list will give them one or two achievable items on which to focus for a limited amount of time. Model editing for these specific skills first, and then have them continue on their own. Hold them accountable for catching all or most of the targeted errors. Repeat at a later time.
- Allow students to edit in a new color. This will highlight where they edited for you and make it more focused and fun for them.

5. In Section 6, we provide an editing checklist. Choose one or two skills to assign to a student to focus on, according to what they need the most practice on. It makes sense to choose skills around which a student has some understanding but not full mastery yet.

Avoid skills that are already mastered or still beyond reach. The Persuasive Writing COPS Editing Checklist on page 116 is designed for students to use. Customize it according to what has been taught to students. At grades 3–5, it is recommended to begin using this type of checklist in a conference between a teacher and a student and to then gradually help students build independence so they can use them on their own.

Promoting Strong Persuasive Writing *(cont.)*

Strategy 21: Writers publish and share opinions with an authentic audience.

EXPLANATION

This strategy provides suggestions for how students can publish and share their work with an authentic audience. Our goal is to ensure that students view their work as purposeful and having a place in the world. We hope that as students find their views on a topic and the courage to express their voice, their work is not being filed in a writing portfolio and taken out only during writing conferences but being shared meaningfully. As often as possible, we want to find ways to share our students' writing in authentic ways. It also ensures that students are given the time and the necessary support to bring their projects to completion and are able to proudly show off their hard work. Students will work harder if they know that their work is valued, honored, and celebrated. The goal of this book is for students to become critical thinkers who read persuasive messages with an informed eye and to become creators of their own strong and effective persuasive messages. And now in this strategy, we want students to learn how to express their views with confidence, pride, and joy. In Strategy 13, we asked students to think carefully about their audience beyond their teacher. We asked students to consider who would be their best audience and what would be the most effective form of writing to reach that audience. In this strategy, we ask students to carry out the act of sharing their work in order to reach their audience. Different writing pieces lend themselves to different ways of sharing, and it is up to you, their teacher, to determine the right audience and best method for this.

SUPPORT FOR THE STRATEGY

1. Provide students with ample time to publish their work. A piece ready for publication will look different for each student, but we must honor their hard work and provide support, when necessary, as they make their finishing touches.

2. Look at Strategy 13, and make sure that students have a strong foundation in understanding the concept of audience and that they understand that the purpose of persuasive writing is to get their audience to act or think in a particular way.

3. Find ways to connect students to an authentic audience. Ideally, this audience will be composed of someone who can make a difference or who deeply cares about the topic.
   - Schedule a community meeting, and invite the principal, families, or community members into the classroom to listen to students share their opinion on relevant topics.
   - Create a *My View, My Voice* class blog on a platform like KidBlog.com or on a class website, and have students publish their pieces online, providing them with time to add comments and read the comments of others. Share the blog with people who may be influenced by the opinions.
   - Set up Skype, Voxer, or FaceTime calls with relevant audiences (classes in another school, local leaders, etc.).
   - Find a class in another community (or country) to become ePals with. Choose a topic that is relevant to both classroom communities (e.g., the environment), and have students share their published pieces among the two communities.
   - Find a place besides the classroom wall to share students' work: local stores or shops, a community wall outside the school, and other venues that are connected to their topics.

Promoting Strong Persuasive Writing *(cont.)*

4. Create a class chart titled "How to Share My View with Pride." The chart may look like:

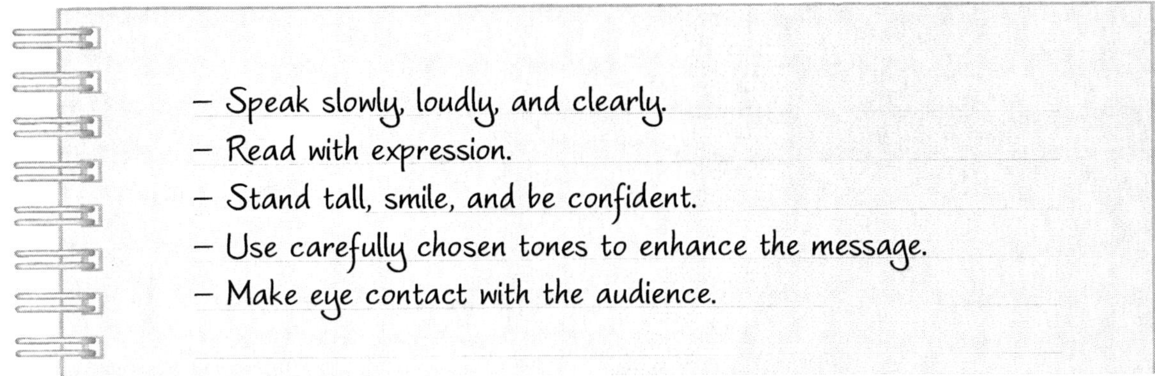

5. Make sure students are really ready before they share their pieces. Model reading a piece aloud, emphasizing *how* to share the piece with pride. Provide students with ample time to practice sharing their pieces, first with partners and then with small groups. Have students whose home language is not English present their pieces in their home language.

6. We also must ensure that our students feel safe and honored as they share their work. This requires establishing a respectful protocol for students when they voice their views, such as:
   - Listen with care.
   - Be kind, and honor all opinions.
   - Come up with one thing you love about each piece (e.g., the opinion, the evidence).

SECTION 4

Questions for Professional Growth

- Which of the 21 Strategies are you currently addressing as part of your writing instruction? Which feel like uncharted territory?
- Choose three strategies that you would like to implement in the near future. Why did you choose those three?
- How do these strategies differ from the way you currently teach persuasive writing or were taught yourself? Would successful achievement of these strategies produce different results than the methods with which you are familiar? If so, how do you anticipate that outcomes would be different for students?
- What do you think is the most important strategy of all? Why? (No right answers—just good thinking needed!)
- Discuss which strategies feel most like a stretch for some or all of your students. What accommodations might you provide to help students be successful?
- How would becoming a successful persuasive writer benefit your students at their age now? In the future?

Model Lessons

"The moment we begin to fear the opinions of others and hesitate to tell the truth that is in us, and from motives of policy are silent when we should speak, the divine floods of light and life no longer flow into our souls."

—Elizabeth Cady Stanton

Overview

Every *My View, My Voice: 21 Strategies for Powerful, Persuasive Writing* model lesson provides a clear teaching objective, an explanation, and a materials list to aid teacher planning and preparation.

Lesson Design

The 10 model lessons are designed using a gradual release of responsibility framework—a carefully planned sequence of *Model*, *Coach*, *Practice*, and *Closure*. The purpose of this sequence is to help students build independence and confidence in their own capacities to implement the target strategy. This sequence ensures that for each strategy, students will know what to do and how to do it by the end of the lesson.

The segments of the *My View, My Voice* lessons are:

Model—The students view their teacher's expert demonstration of what they need to understand and do.

Coach—The students try out what they need to know, often with partners, under the watchful eye and guidance of the teacher.

Practice—The students apply their knowledge independently, with the teacher acting as facilitator. This is the longest segment of the lesson, typically taking about twice the time as the other segments combined.

Closure—The students may engage in any or all of the following: sharing their work, reflecting on their successes, and articulating the purposes of their learning.

It is strongly recommended to teach all four segments and use this structure to plan lessons around the remaining strategies in this book.

Model Lesson A

Strategy 1

Writers explore the relationship between fact and opinion.

Purpose

The purpose of this lesson is for students to look closely at persuasive texts to analyze the relationship between facts and opinions in the text. Students will be asked to look at the opinion statement or claim and think about how the author may have used facts to help form the opinion. Students will also be asked to notice how the author uses facts to support the opinion. There is a set of four questions to help guide students' analysis. This lesson is a good foundation to use when asking students to evaluate the soundness of an argument and when asking to provide facts (evidence) to support their reasoning.

Materials

- enlarged version of "Art Class Is a Necessity Version 1" or "Art Class Is a Necessity Version 2" (pages 145–146) for modeling
- student copies of "Toyland Advertisement" (page 160) or "Why Maya Angelou Inspires Me" (page 153) for practice

SECTION 5

Procedure

Model

1. Review the definitions of the terms *fact* and *opinion* (see Strategy 1 in Section 4). If students still struggle to recognize the difference between a fact and an opinion, take the time to go through the support for Strategy 1.
2. Explain that the goal of this lesson is to be able to recognize how facts and opinions work together to form a strong persuasive piece. Students will look at how authors often use facts when they are forming their opinion or claim and to support their opinions and claims.
3. Introduce (or review) the following questions. Explain that by closely reading a text, students can analyze how the author uses facts and opinions. Share the following questions with students, and take the time to make sure that students understand them.
    - What is the topic or issue?
    - What is the author's opinion(s) related to the topic? How do you know?
    - Does the author include facts? How do the facts help the author prove his point?
    - What things does the author say that can be proven to be true? What things are arguable?
4. Choose a text to read aloud for modeling, such as "Art Class Is a Necessity Version 1." Take students through all four of the questions, and think out loud about the connection between facts and opinion.

Coach

1. Break students up into partnerships or small groups. Introduce a second opinion text to students. "Toyland Advertisement" or "Why Maya Angelou Inspires Me" could work. Explain that they will use the first two questions from above to analyze the relationship between facts and options in opinion texts.

2. Once students have had enough time to read the text and answer the first two questions, reconvene as a whole class and review their answers.

Practice

1. Independently, have students continue with the same sample text and answer the remaining two questions about the text. Circulate the room to support students, or work in small groups to reinforce the concept. You may wish to have other opinion pieces available for students to work on if they complete the first one.

Closure

1. Gather the class and reread the sample text. Have volunteers explore the relationship between facts and opinion. Discuss how the facts help support the opinion and how, as an author, you can use facts to formulate your own opinion or claim.

2. Remind students that when they read persuasive writing, it is important to notice how authors use facts and opinions.

Differentiation

1. If these are new or challenging concepts for your class, take time to ensure that students are really able to identify facts and opinions in texts. Spend a few days diagramming opinion texts, highlighting the opinions in red and the facts in green. Such visual color coding will help ELs and other students grasp the concept.

2. If some students cannot read the texts independently for Independent Practice, make the text accessible to them by reading it aloud first, working in partnerships or small groups, or providing students with a recorded text.

Section 6 provides texts at a variety of levels to facilitate differentiation. Any may be used for practice of this lessons objective.

Model Lesson B

Strategy 3

Writers analyze the elements of persuasive writing.

Purpose

Becoming strong, analytical readers of persuasive text will help students become stronger writers of persuasive text. This lesson engages students in reading persuasive text in search of key elements of the genre. This work helps to lay a foundational understanding of the elements and academic language they can use in their own persuasive writing.

Materials

- enlarged version of "Summer Vacation Is Important Version 2" (pages 149–150)
- student copies of *Get Up! Get Out!* (page 157)
- student copies of *Art Class Is a Necessity Version 1* (pages 145)
- colored markers (or digital pen) to annotate the text

SECTION 5

Procedure

Model

1. Discuss the term *persuade* with students. Explain that to persuade is to try to convince others to believe something or act in a certain way. Ask, "How many of you have ever tried to persuade a parent to let you stay up longer? Did you convince them? How?"
2. Explain that when we try to persuade others, we usually do these things: share our opinions on a topic; provide reasons why other people should agree with and/or act on our opinion; and add evidence that explains and backs up our reasons.
3. Connect the following with the discussion in Step 1:
    - Topic: staying up late
    - Opinion: I believe I should stay up late tonight.
    - Reason 1: I am not tired.
    - Evidence 1: See, I am full of energy! I got plenty of sleep last night!
    - Reason 2: I have a special show I want to watch.
    - Evidence: The last episode of my favorite superhero series is on. I have been waiting to watch it for three weeks! I cannot wait!
4. Model using an informational opinion piece in which the author addresses a familiar topic or issue, such as "Summer Vacation Is Important 2." Read the text aloud to the class. Then, think aloud about the elements of the text: topic, opinion, reasons, and evidence. Actively search for common clues that may point to the elements, such as the title, location in the text, and academic phrases such as *It is clear that...*, or *Another reason is...* Use a colored marker to annotate the text as you identify the elements.

- Note that in authentic persuasive texts (e.g., real-world writing), elements such as the opinion statement, reasons, and evidence are not always presented in clean paragraphs with clear topic sentences that are followed neatly by supporting details. Sometimes, the reader must synthesize and make inferences to determine what the author's reasoning is.
- Say, "I see that most of the sentences in this piece are about summer vacation, so that must be the topic. The title talks about the importance of summer vacation, so that is a very strong clue that the author is going to write about why summer vacation is important. Let's look at the first paragraph. The writer introduces the question of getting rid of summer vacation in schools. That is the topic for sure. Then, the writer hopes this does not happen and ends the paragraph with this sentence 'Summer vacation is important to kids for a lot of reasons.' That sounds like the main opinion right there. Writers do not always put the main opinion in the last line of the first paragraph, but this time, she did. I bet the author is going to give some reasons next."
- Reiterate that people strengthen their arguments by providing reasons and evidence to support their opinions. Return to "Summer Vacation Is Important Version 2" to find reasons to support the opinion and evidence, or proof. Explain and support the reasons in the form of examples, description, facts, stories, or quotes from experts.
- Say, "Look carefully for reasons that the author provides to support her opinion. In the second paragraph, the author says that without summer vacation, she will not have enough time with family. Then, she provides a personal example and an explanation as evidence. ' In order to get proper recreation and the chance to spend time with brothers and sisters, it is necessary for students to be out of school for an extended period of time. In my case, I do not get to spend time with my little brother while I am in school. After school, I need to study and complete my homework. Then, my parents make me eat dinner, and pretty soon I need to sleep for the next day. If I do not have summer vacation, then I do not have any significant time to play with my brother.'"
- Continue with the remainder of the text. Model annotating the text, identifying the opinion, the reasons, and evidence.

Coach

1. Repeat with another piece of persuasive writing in a different form, such as the infographic *Get Up! Get Out!* (page 157).
2. Have students work in pairs to identify the topic and opinion. Topic: being active in the summer. Opinion: It is important for kids to be active in the summer. Then, have students find reasons and evidence in the piece. Support students in navigating this genre. An infographic often requires some inferring. For example, in this sample, it's the factual evidence. Some reasons for kids to be active that the students may infer:
    - Kids who are active will be healthier.
    - Kids need more exercise.
    - Kids spend too much time in front of televisions.
    - There are a lot of popular sports to play in the summer.
    - There are a lot of fun things to do in the summer, even if you cannot get outside.

Practice

Students work with partners to read another short opinion piece, such as "Art Class Is a Necessity Version 1." Partners focus on identifying the topic, opinion, reasons, and evidence being expressed by the author. Have them annotate the text to indicate the topic, opinion, reasons, and evidence.

Closure

Gather the class and reread "Art Class Is a Necessity Version 1." Have volunteers identify the topic, opinion, reasons, and evidence in the piece, annotating the text in the process.

Differentiation

1. If these are new or challenging concepts for your class, separate the strands of the strategy into separate lessons. Focus on identifying opinion in the first lesson and reasons and evidence in the second lesson.
2. If some students cannot read the texts independently for independent practice, make the text accessible by reading it aloud first, working in pairs or small groups, or providing students with a recorded text. Section 6 provides texts at a variety of levels in Section 6 to facilitate differentiation. Any text may be used for practice of this lesson's objective.

Model Lesson C

Strategy 4

Writers examine the techniques that strengthen persuasive writing.

Purpose

This lesson introduces three persuasive techniques that date back to the writings of Aristotle. It builds students' awareness of how writers use these techniques to influence the views of others. Such awareness will help them become more savvy consumers of persuasive text and enhance their persuasion tool kits. The teacher provides illustrative examples of technique, and the students examine persuasive pieces in a variety of genres to analyze how the writer employs the techniques. For practice, students explore a variety of persuasive text samples in search of how writers use each of the three techniques.

Materials

- student copies of *Aristotle's Many Ways to Persuade Bookmark* (page 117)
- student copies of "Save the Tigers" for modeling (page 141)
- student copies of "Head to the Hut" (pages 138–139)
- a variety of persuasive texts for practice

Procedure

Model

1. Tell students that you are going to teach them about three tools that people have been using to persuade others for thousands of years and that are still being used today.
2. Present the "Save the Tigers" opinion piece, and read it aloud with a lot of expression.
3. Ask students to turn and talk to each other:
   - What opinions do you notice in the piece?
   - What does the writer want others to do (call to action)?
4. Clarify that the purpose of the piece is to persuade people to help save tigers. Present student copies of the bookmark from page 117 that displays three ways that writers persuade others. Explain the first one. (There are illustrative examples on page 49, if you need them.) Point out the icon to remind them what the technique is about.
5. Here are some simple explanations that students in grades 3–5 can understand:

   Ethos *is when a writer shows that he or she (or the source of information) knows a lot about the topic to get the reader to believe the writer's ideas.*

   Pathos *is when the writer talks about his or her feelings or tries to stir the reader's feelings to make the reader care more about the topic.*

   Logos *is when the writer includes facts to help convince the reader that what he or she says is true.*
6. Reread the sample piece with students, and look for evidence of the focus technique in the sample piece. Have them turn and talk with partners to speculate where they think the evidence is. This particular piece has evidence of the writer attempting to use all three. If the students cannot find the evidence, help them.

7. Repeat with all three techniques. Below are sentences that represent each technique.

   Ethos: Mention knowledgeable sources: *The World Wildlife Foundation, a group that works to save endangered animals, says on its website...*

   Pathos: Statements that tap the readers' emotions: *Tigers are amazing animals. It is tragic that there are not as many tigers as there used to be in the world.*

   Logos: Facts that show how tigers are amazing and worth saving; facts that show that tigers are really in danger and that humans can make a difference: *There are only about 3,200 tigers left in the world.*

Coach

1. Hand out copies of *Aristotle's Many Ways to Persuade Bookmark* (page 117), and review its content with the students.
2. Provide students with another persuasive sample that uses one or more of Aristotle's three techniques, such as "Head to the Hut" (pages 138–139) to annotate.

Practice

1. Provide a short packet of additional examples of persuasive texts for analysis, using samples of your choice from the back of this book as well as texts you have selected to match your students' needs and interests. Have students choose pieces to read and view, searching for examples of writers who use ethos, pathos, and logos techniques to strengthen their persuasive messages.
2. Confer with students to support them in their searches. Ask questions, such as:
   - What examples of ethos, pathos, and logos have you found?
   - What makes you say that this is an example of ethos/pathos/logos?
   - Ethos: Does the writer seem to be an expert on the topic? Is there an expert or a respected figure included to impress the audience? Does the information come from a reputable source?
   - Pathos: Does anything in this text try to make the audience experience an emotion? Does the writer use powerful words to stir the audience's feelings?
   - Logos: Does the writer use facts, examples, or description to prove his points?

Closure

Have some volunteers share their findings. Celebrate students' attempts to find evidence of ethos, pathos, and logos.

Differentiation

1. Introduce ethos, pathos, and logos in three different lessons if introducing them all in one lesson seems like too much.
2. Use a variety of text levels, including student-composed samples and visual texts, such as ads and posters, for analysis.

Model Lesson D

Strategy 6

Writers consider multiple viewpoints on an issue.

Purpose

This lesson encourages students to examine various sides of a topic. There are multiple viewpoints that show the impact of seeing things from more than one point of view.

Materials

- chart paper and markers for modeling
- crayons
- list of topics for students to choose from

Procedure

Model

1. Tell the class that you and your friends have been holding a debate about an important topic. What's a debate? A debate is a discussion between people in which they express different opinions about something. You and your friends have been debating about whether third graders should be assigned homework. Quickly poll the class: "Raise your hand if you think teachers should stop giving homework."

2. Discuss the results of your poll with the class. Ask those who raised their hands why they did so. Chart the reasonings under the heading *No Homework*. Then, ask those who did not raise their hands to explain their reasoning. Chart these under *Yes Homework*. (Do this swiftly. Do not discriminate between reasons and evidence in this lesson.) If no one voted for keeping homework, prompt students to suggest some reasoning that homework is a good practice so you have both pros and cons listed.

3. Explain that when you debated homework with your friends, the same thing happened. Some people were for homework, and some were against. Draw a horizontal line, and label one end *No Homework* and the other end *Yes Homework*. Draw a star on each end of the line to indicate people with views on each end.

4. Draw another star somewhere in the middle of the line. Ask students to turn and respond as you say: "Why do you think I drew a star there in the center?" If necessary, guide students to understand that some people felt strongly for or against homework and they are represented by the stars on either end, but some people saw good reasons for *and* against homework, so their views were somewhere in between (the star in the middle).

Model Lesson D *(cont.)*

Coach

1. Have students turn and talk about where their stars would go. Quickly, ask two or three students to add stars to the chart that represents their feelings about homework. Guide them to place their star anywhere on the continuum.
2. Point out to students that you did not give them much time to think deeply about why teachers should or should not give homework. When forming a view about a complicated issue such as this, it is important to think critically about the reasoning and evidence on each side. Revisit the Yes and No reasoning listed earlier. As a class, add ideas to the *No Homework* side, and then add ideas to the *Yes Homework* side.
3. Ask students if this additional discussion caused anyone to change where his or her stars go. Ask volunteers to explain why or why not. Point out that people often change their views in light of new reasons and evidence.

Practice

1. Divide students into groups of two to four. Choose topics from the list below, writing them on sheets of paper to hand out to each group. Insert opposing views on the ends of a continuum, as you modeled. It is best to use topics with clear opposing views that are familiar to students to argue for either side. This will be based on background knowledge only because there is no time to research the topic in the lesson. Some topic suggestions are:
    - football is the best sport versus basketball is the best sport
    - city life is the best versus country life is the best
    - television is good for kids versus television is bad for kids
    - video games are good for kids versus video games are bad for kids
    - students should learn cursive writing versus students should not learn cursive writing
    - there should be school uniforms versus there should not be school uniforms
    - students should have homework versus students should not have homework
    - physical education should be mandatory versus physical education should be optional
    - school should be year-round versus school should not be year-round
    - school days should be short versus school days should not be short
    - technology is distracting versus technology is beneficial

Rating, Reasoning, Reflection

1. Rating: Before any discussions, each group member should use a crayon to put a colored star on the line that marks where he or she stands in this debate.
2. Reasoning: With your team, record as much reasoning for both views as you can. Even if you strongly agree with one side, do your best to think about how the other side may think.
3. Reflection: After you complete item two, think about where your star would go now. Each group member should use a different-color crayon to mark his or her view now.
4. Discuss: Was it hard or easy to think of reasons for both sides? Why? Did your star move after you discussed reasons for both sides of the debate? If so, what changed? Why? If not, why not?

2. Guide students through the directions, providing as much structure as needed.
3. Option: Have groups discuss the questions under Step 4 independently and share during the conclusion of the lesson. Or hold a whole group discussion during the conclusion of the lesson.

Closure

Have students share their responses to the discussion questions from Step 4 on the Rating, Reasoning, Reflection for Dogs versus Cats as the Best Pets.

Differentiation

1. When discussing opposing views on a topic, be dramatic, using plenty of facial expression and body language to emphasize the meaning of what you say. Use visual images to represent topics as well (e.g., images of basketball and football or images of a city scene and a country scene). This will help ELs better comprehend the topics and reasoning.
2. Provide extended wait time when you prompt students to articulate their views and reasoning. This is great for ELs in particular, because it gives them a chance to figure out their answers *and* find the words to express them.
3. Some students may be extreme in their views and have trouble seeing things through the eyes of others. Provide context for their thinking. For example, say things such as, "I want you to think for a moment like a teacher would. A teacher wants students to learn and to be safe. What might a teacher think here?"

Model Lesson E

Strategy 7

Writers evaluate the strength of reasoning in persuasive pieces.

Purpose

Reasoning is one's logical thinking about an issue to draw a conclusion or make a judgment. Reasoning can also mean the reasons and evidence that result from the thinking process. Students will learn to evaluate the evidence and the reasons to determine whether the reasoning is solid. Solid reasoning means that one's evidence and supporting reasons are logical, relevant, and credible. Students will be asked to slow down as they closely read persuasive messages. They will look at the evidence and the reasons and determine whether it is sound.

Materials

- copies of *Soundness of Reasons and Evidence* graphic organizer (pages 113–114). **Note:** There are two versions of this graphic organizer provided. Option 1 is simpler, whereas Option 2 is for students with more background knowledge and strong analytical abilities.
- copies of "Students in Year-Round Schooling Are Ahead Version 1" or "Students in Year-Round Schooling Are Ahead Version 2" (pages 150–151)
- copies of "The Importance of Owning a Dog" (page 140)

SECTION 5

Procedure

Model

1. Make sure that students have a clear understanding of the terms *reasons*, *evidence*, and *reasoning*. For support, see Strategy 7.
2. Define the term *solid reasoning* (when one's reasons and evidence are logical, relevant, and credible), and explicitly explain and discuss what it means for a supporting reason to be logical, relevant, and credible. Say, "When we talk about solid reasoning, we are looking for clues that tell us, the reader, that the evidence the author uses makes sense, directly relates to the opinion, and is convincing and believable."
3. If students need additional practice recognizing sound reasoning, refer back to Strategy 7 for support.
4. Explain to students that the focus of this lesson will be learning *how* to evaluate the strength of reasoning. Introduce students to one of the two *Soundness of Reasons and Evidence* graphic organizer options. The first option requires students to identify the opinion and reasoning as part of the task. The second option assumes that students can analyze those elements without the scaffolding of a graphic organizer, focusing solely on evaluative criteria.
5. Model how to use the graphic organizer best suited to your class's needs (for the purpose of modeling, we use Option 1). Choose a sample text, such as "Students in Year-Round Schooling Are Ahead Version 1." A completed version is on page 115. In front of the class, record your answers to all but the final two questions on the graphic organizer. Explain that students will discuss and record the answers to those questions during the Coach segment of the lesson.

Coach

1. Put students into small groups. Explain that students will discuss their answers to the final two questions on the graphic organizer and record their thinking.
2. Ask, "Did the author confirm or change your thinking? How?"
3. Say, "On a scale of 1 to 10 (with 10 being the most persuasive), how strong is this persuasive piece? Explain your answer."
4. Return to a whole-class discussion, and have students share their responses to the final two questions. Evaluate as a whole what students felt about the strength of reasoning in the piece. Were they convinced? If so, what was most effective? If not, what might have changed their minds?

Practice

1. Provide students with a second persuasive piece, "The Importance of Owning a Dog," and their own copies of the Soundness of Reasons and Evidence graphic organizers. Provide students with sufficient time to read the new piece and answer the questions to determine the soundness of reasoning.
2. Circulate the room, supporting students as they evaluate the strength or reasoning in the piece.

Closure

Select several students to share their answers to each of the questions. As a class, evaluate the piece's soundness of reasoning.

Differentiation

1. Conduct a shared reading of the persuasive pieces, and have students work with partners to address the questions on the graphic organizer.
2. Allow students to work with partners or small groups to complete their graphic organizers.
3. Encourage students to orally rehearse their thoughts with partners prior to writing.

Model Lesson F

Strategy 9

Writers use conversation to develop their ideas.

Purpose

This lesson introduces simple ground rules for productive student-to-student conversation and emphasizes the benefits of talking to others as a way to explore and develop one's views on topics. The focus of this lesson is establishing the behaviors necessary to successfully participate in a group conversation.

Materials

- a list of topics of interest to students (see Strategies 5 and 6 for topic ideas, if needed.)
- charting supplies to create a chart titled *How to Have a Good Conversation*

SECTION 5

Procedure

Before teaching this lesson, arrange students into discussion groups of four or five students. Students will work in these small groups to discuss their opinions on topics of interest.

Model

1. Inform students that they will each be crafting short pieces about their opinions or claims to share with the world. Explain that before putting their opinions or claims in writing, people often discuss their opinions with others. Listening to others' information may help strengthen their opinions or claims. Say, "When you talk to other people about your opinion or claim, you may discover that they have something to share that will help you make your claim even stronger. Maybe they have an idea for another reason to support your opinion, or they may help you to think about the topic you are focusing on in a different way. Either way, talking about your opinions with others will only help make your writing stronger."

2. Model choosing a topic from your list, and state an opinion and a reason. Say, "One of the topics I care about is making healthy choices. I think that our cafeteria should serve more fresh fruits and vegetables. One reason is that fruits and vegetables are delicious! I would want to talk with you all today. I bet I would learn something by doing that. But first, let's talk about how to have a good conversation."

3. Begin a chart titled *How to Have a Good Conversation*. Explain to the class that having a good conversation means following specific rules for how to behave.

How to Have a Good Conversation

- Listen with care.
- Take turns.
- Stay on topic.

Coach

1. Model how to choose a topic (use the topic list in Strategy 5 for support), and share an opinion or a claim and supporting reasons. Ask the group members to share their thinking about the stated opinion or claim. Model following each of the rules listed, and/or point out moments in which other students are demonstrating following these rules. Encourage students to agree or disagree and explain their thinking. They may also add to the discussion with new reasoning, observations, or other information.
2. Use the following prompts to guide the conversation:
   - What is your opinion?
   - What reasoning do you have to support the opinion?
   - Do you agree with this opinion? Why?
   - Do you disagree with this opinion? Why?
3. Consider role-playing what it looks like to *not* follow a particular rule. For example, as the conversation proceeds, begin to actively *not* listen to the conversation. Stop the role-playing, and turn to the class, asking for suggestions of how to get the conversation back on track.
4. Reflect on the conversation, and explain specific ways the conversation helped grow your thinking about the topic.

Practice

1. Direct students to meet in their discussion groups. They should choose a topic from the list to discuss (or, if necessary, assign them a topic). Then, they should take turns expressing opinions and reasoning on the topic and responding to each other.
2. Circulate the room to coach conversations. Gather examples of good work to share during the closure of the lesson.

Closure

1. Showcase examples of productive conversations you overheard.
2. Ask students to share their conversations. Ask, "How did talking help you today? Was it hard to follow our rules for conversations? Why? What can we do about it next time?"

Differentiation

1. Some students may need more support with what to say and ask during a collaborative conversation. Provide practice using simple conversation prompts and questions. ELs in particular will benefit from the scaffold these sentence stems provide. The frames help them see what forms English speakers use to accomplish the linguistic actions of *agreeing, disagreeing,* and *clarifying*. Here are some samples:

   A Conversation Builders
   - I agree with _____ because _____.
   - I disagree with _____ because _____.
   - I would like to add that _____.

   B Helping Questions
   - What did you mean by _____?
   - Can you say more about _____?
2. Pair students strategically: bilingual peers may be able to help ELs by using their home language as a resource in these conversations. Pair a shy student with someone who is more outgoing but not necessarily the most outspoken in the class.
3. Occasionally interrupt the conversations to showcase specific examples of productive conversation to the entire class.
4. Be patient. The class may only be able to handle one or two minutes of discussion at this point if they do not often converse in this way. Focus on modeling and coaching positive behavior and growing stamina over time.

Model Lesson G

Strategy 11

Writers provide evidence to support reasons.

Purpose

In this lesson, students will provide three reasons and evidence to support their reasons.

Materials

- student copies of the *What I Think and Why* graphic organizer (page 118)
- the topic list in Strategy 5
- resources for finding evidence (see Modeling Step 3)

SECTION 5

Procedure

Model

1. Make sure that students have a solid understanding of reasons and evidence (see Strategy 11 for more support). A *reason* is a cause, an explanation, or a justification for an event, an action, an opinion, or a claim. *Evidence*, or proof, is information that verifies the truth of something. Evidence backs the reason. Say, "For example, *trees are important.* (opinion) *Trees provide oxygen, which humans need to breathe.* (reason) *According to TreePeople.org, 'In one year, an acre of mature trees can provide enough oxygen for 18 people.'*" (evidence)
2. Hold a discussion about where persuasive writers can find evidence.
3. Facts and statistics examples (best if the source is provided):
   - anecdotes (e.g., a story that backs a point)
   - sensory details or description (see, hear, smell, taste, feel)
   - expert opinion or testimonials
   - quotations from credible texts/sources

   Say, "We can find evidence to support our reasons in many places. The list above describes the types of evidence we can use, but sometimes it can be tricky to know where to look to find the evidence. For example, if I were writing a persuasive piece on why everyone should see a particular movie, what resources could I use to find evidence? I could read about how the movie is doing—how many people went to see it on opening weekend, I could use examples from the movie itself, I could describe how the movie made me feel, I could read a review of the movie in my local newspaper, or I could interview a friend who has also seen the movie. Sometimes, we have to be creative when finding evidence, but the search can be fun!"

4. Introduce students to the *What I Think and Why* graphic organizer. Display a copy of the graphic organizer, and demonstrate how to fill it in using a topic and an opinion of your choosing. If desired, repeat the experience with more than one opinion so that students can see different examples of how to find and use evidence to support their reasons.

Coach

Have students choose their topics. Refer students to the topic list in Strategy 5 for support. In pairs, they should discuss what the topic is and where they may find information about the topic (e.g., Who could they interview or poll? What book, magazine, or website might they read?) Before sending students off to work with their partners, remind them of the resources you might turn to if you were writing a piece on trees. Say, "If I wanted to write a piece on trees, I might first read an informational book about trees. I then might interview someone such as my uncle, who is a tree doctor, or I might look at a website about trees."

Practice

1. Students work independently to research the topic, develop their opinions, and find reasons and evidence to support their opinions.
2. Students record their thinking on the *What I Think and Why* graphic organizer.
3. Circulate the room to meet with students, and provide support as needed.

Closure

Gather the class and ask students to share their reasons and evidence with partners.

Differentiation

1. Students often jump to conclusions about a topic and form opinions and reasons that are not based on evidence. Then, when they seek evidence, either it does not exist or it contradicts their thinking. Some stubbornly cling to their misguided conclusions, leading to poorly supported claims in writing. Teach students to look objectively at evidence and be flexible about modifying their opinions and reasoning.
2. Frequently check students' organizers to be sure that they are not confusing reasons and evidence. Some of the confusion stems from a need to better understand the concepts of *general* and *specific*. Reasons should be general explanations of the main opinion; evidence is specific support for those reasons. For example, in a piece about smoking, students might find the fact *Nine out of 10 lung cancer deaths are caused by smoking* and want to provide this as a reason instead of using a general statement such as *Smoking is bad for people's health.*
3. Consider having students use note cards to gather facts on their topics, one fact per card. Then, they can easily sort their cards into similar clusters that match up with their reasons. Evaluate which reasons are lacking support, or use their piles of facts to determine what their reasons should be.

Model Lesson H

Strategy 14

Writers use effective words and phrases to connect ideas.

Purpose

In this lesson, students will be asked to use effective words and phrases to connect ideas. They will practice by writing short persuasive pieces.

Materials

- student copies of an opinion paragraph with examples of linking words and phrases that join ideas and sections, such as "The Importance of Owning a Dog" (page 140)
- writing paper for students to write their own opinion pieces
- student copies of *Common Linking Words and Phrases* (page 119)

SECTION 5

Procedure

Model

1. Introduce the term *linking words and phrases*, clearly explaining their purposes. Linking words and phrases join together ideas (e.g., *because*, *and*, *also*, *another*).
    - Example: *I think I should get a dog because dogs are great companions.*
    - Example: *For example, I could take a dog on a walk so both of us get exercise.*
    - Example: *Another reason is that owning a dog can teach responsibility.*
2. Read aloud an opinion paragraph with examples of linking words, separating the opinion from reasons, such as "The Importance of Owning a Dog." Underline the opinion in one color and the reasons in another color. Circle the linking words and phrases. Discuss how the author uses linking words to make the writing smooth and clear.
3. Model how to choose a topic, and then model how to write an opinion statement on the topic (e.g., *I think our school is a great school.*). Think aloud about reasons that may support your opinion. (e.g., *Our school has outstanding teachers. We have excellent facilities and materials. We have many extracurricular activities. Students are happy here.*) Then, demonstrate how to turn opinion and supporting reasons into an opinion paragraph (or multiple paragraphs, if you prefer) using linking words to connect ideas. Your example may look like the one on the following page:

Example Opinion Paragraph

Warren William Memorial School is a fantastic school! One reason is that we have outstanding teachers. Our teachers care about student learning. They meet together regularly to plan the best lessons possible. Furthermore, we have excellent facilities and materials. We just built a new science lab and a nature courtyard outside for students to study in. In addition, we have beautiful books and computers in every classroom. Also, we have many extracurricular activities. For example, we have a choir, instrumental music, and an intramural sports program that anyone can join. Finally, our students are happy here. We have a culture in which teachers and students respect each other and work together. Our motto is "Kindness Counts," and our school community lives up to that. As a result, both adults and students feel good about coming to our school. We love Warren William Memorial!

Note: Caution students to not use reasons in their main opinion statements. "Warren William Memorial is a fantastic school because it has outstanding teachers" is not an effective opener because it limits the focus to the teachers only. Keep the opinion general: "Warren William Memorial is a fantastic school."

Coach

1. Students choose familiar topics they would like to write opinion paragraphs (or multiparagraph essays) about and share the topics with partners.
2. In pairs, have students generate opinions on the topic and a list of possible reasons to support their opinions.
3. Students look at the list of *Common Linking Words* and Phrases and choose some words and phrases they would like to try to use in their opinion paragraphs.

Practice

Students use the opinion and supporting reasons generated during the Coaching segment of the lesson to write opinion paragraphs on topics of their choosing. They use Common Linking Words and Phrases to join their ideas.

Closure

Select several students to read their paragraphs aloud. Have students find the linking words and phrases.

Differentiation

1. Emergent writers may dictate their ideas, but they should still practice using the linking words orally.
2. If necessary, reduce the number of linking words and phrases that you present. A beginner list may only include:
   - One reason is...
   - Another reason is...
   - The most important reason is...
3. Have students talk about their ideas using their hands and fingers. Closed fist: Opinion statement. Fingers: Each reason the writer has to support the opinion.
4. Use mentor writing samples as an inspiration so students can see how other writers have used linking words and phrases.

Model Lesson I

Strategy 15

Writers establish a credible, persuasive voice and tone.

Purpose

This lesson guides students to plan powerful word choices to strengthen their persuasive messages. Students consider their opinions and reasoning and collect relevant adjectives that evoke strong images and emotions to include in their writing.

Materials

- a sample writing piece that uses powerful adjectives, such as "Head to the Hut" (pages 138–139)
- a thesaurus for every student
- students' writing in progress

SECTION 5

Procedure

Model

1. Display the following sentence pairs on the board:
    - *If we all do not stop polluting, it will be bad for the Earth* and *If we all do not stop polluting, it will be devastating to the Earth.*
    - *Try the pizza at Anthony's. It is good* and *Try the pizza at Anthony's. It is scrumptious.*
2. Ask students to turn to a partner and talk about which sentence in each pair is more persuasive and why. They may conclude that the second example in each pair uses powerful adjectives to tap the readers' emotions (*devastating*) or senses (*scrumptious*). These choices are more effective than *bad* or *good*.
3. Explain that using powerful adjectives can help a writer be more persuasive. Tell students to listen carefully for powerful adjectives in a piece as you read. They should give a thumbs-up when they hear an adjective that describes a strong image (sight, sound, taste, smell, etc.) or stirs an emotion (fear, excitement, sadness, etc.). Explain that using such words can help make a piece more persuasive. Display and read the first paragraph of the piece "Head to the Hut." Dramatically emphasize the adjectives (*delicious, fine, brilliant, silky, outstanding, delightful*) to scaffold students' ability to detect them. Assign a scribe, if possible, to chart the adjectives as you and the class discover them. Read the whole list together chorally, taking a second to briefly clarify the meaning of challenging words, if needed.

Coach

1. Model how to plan a list of powerful word choices to match the focus of your writing. Write the heading *Awesome Adjectives* on a chart or board. Say, "I need to start by thinking about my piece and the point I am trying to make. Let's say I am trying to persuade my audience to go to The Seafood Hut restaurant. It is a really pretty

restaurant with great service and food. I can plan positive words that can describe those things."

2. Model how to generate a list of powerful adjectives that match your piece. Show students that when they cannot think of enough words on their own, they can use a thesaurus or an online synonym search for more ideas. They should start with a simple word, such as *good* or *pretty*, and use the thesaurus to generate more sophisticated words. Explain that later you can use this pre-planned list as a menu to compose or revise your piece.

Awesome Adjectives

delicious	top-notch
gorgeous	spectacular
amazing	dazzling

3. Reiterate the concept of matching the list to the piece itself. If a student were writing a piece that warns against the negative effects of bullying, the list would be quite different. Have students talk to their partner about adjectives that may be effective in that piece. Chart their responses. If desired, model using a thesaurus or an online search to find more words. Again, it works to start with simple words, such as *mean*, *bad*, and *sad*. This Awesome Adjectives list may include words such as *cruel*, *destructive*, *heartless*, and *miserable*.

Practice

1. Students work on a piece they have in progress to generate their own *Awesome Adjectives* lists. Have students come up with 5 to 10 words to match their persuasive writing.
2. Students use their lists as a menu to compose or revise their pieces. Students do not have to use all of the words they gathered.
3. Circulate the room to confer and support students with the concept.

Closure

Have volunteers share the focus of their pieces, their word lists, and one or two sentences in which they used words from their lists.

Differentiation

1. This lesson does not require prior knowledge of adjectives. The read-aloud modeling is typically enough for students to grasp the concept sufficiently to complete the tasks of the lesson.
2. When possible, help ELs and other students build vocabulary by using body language, facial expressions, and a dramatic voice when saying an adjective. (e.g., Rub your tummy and smile as you say *delicious*.)
3. Students often struggle with making appropriate choices when using a thesaurus. Not all synonyms are created equal—some are too specific or do not quite match the denotation or connotation of the original word. This will be especially challenging for ELs. Expect this, and when you notice a substitution that really does not work, gently guide students to an alternate choice. Reinforce words that work well by saying, "*Scrumptious* is a perfect word to use there!"
4. Work in small groups to develop vocabulary lists with students if they require more intense support.

Model Lesson J

Strategy 17

Writers write structured opinion pieces.

Purpose

The goal of this lesson is for students to write structured opinion pieces with all the necessary components. These components include (at minimum) a clearly stated opinion, logically ordered reasons and evidence to support the opinion, linking words and phrases, a concluding section or sentence that sums up the piece, a call-to-action statement (if relevant).

Most students in grades 3–5 are ready to move on to multi-paragraph writing that contains these components. The structure of the graphic organizer will scaffold their thinking and organization and make it easier to compose multi-paragraph pieces.

Materials

- charting supplies or interactive whiteboard to create a list of components that make a strong opinion piece
- an enlarged and completed version of the *Persuasive Writing Planner* graphic organizer to be used for modeling (see sample on page 107)
- student copies of the *Persuasive Writing Planner* graphic organizer (page 120)

SECTION 5

Procedure

Prior to teaching this lesson, allow students enough time to choose topics and plan their writing by filling in the *Persuasive Writing Planner* graphic organizer. Since the focus of this lesson is on drafting, it is important that students have completed the planning stage first.

Model

1. Create a class chart that lists all components of a strong opinion piece:
    - an opening section that introduces the main opinion or claim
    - body paragraphs that supply logically ordered reasons and evidence
    - linking words and phrases that connect ideas
    - a conclusion that sums up the piece and may contain a call-to-action statement
2. In front of the class, model how to use the ideas in your graphic organizer to write the different components of an opinion piece. Starting with a blank organizer, demonstrate how to plan your ideas using the *Persuasive Writing Planner* organizer (see page 107). Model how to write a sentence that clearly states your opinion or claim.
3. Demonstrate how to write a reason to support the opinion. See Strategy 10 for support.
4. Demonstrate how to provide evidence to support the reason(s). See Strategies 11, 12, and 13 for support.
5. Explain that a conclusion, or concluding statement, often makes a strong recommendation to readers or a call-to-action statement. Model how to craft a concluding statement, using a call-to-action statement.
6. Model how to choose or create relevant illustrations or other visual support. See Strategy 16 for support.

PERSUASIVE WRITING PLANNER	
Main Opinion or Claim: Students should not be reading partners with their friends.	
Reason 1:	One reason is that just because two students are friends does not mean they will like the same books.
Evidence to Support Reason 1:	For example, Erin and Josh are best friends. But Erin likes informational books about dogs, and Josh likes adventure stories.
Reason 2:	Another reason is that sometimes students can be distracted by their friends and not focus on the task.
Evidence to Support Reason 2:	A survey of students in the class showed that 98 percent of them believe that they find it easier to concentrate when they are not near their friends.
Reason 3:	In addition, students can make new friends in class when they have different reading partners.
Evidence to Support Reason 3:	Friends can be found in many places. Think about Clover and Anna in *The Other Side* by Jacqueline Woodson. They may never have been friends if they had not discovered that they both loved sitting on fences. Maybe if you have a reading partner who likes similar books, you could find a new friend, too.
Call to Action: Take a risk! Meet a new friend! Bond over a new favorite book!	

Coach

In pairs, have students use their own *Persuasive Writing Planner* graphic organizers to plan how they are going to draft their opinion pieces.

Practice

Students work independently to draft their own opinion pieces that contain all the required components.

Closure

Select several students to share their pieces, highlighting the required components.

Differentiation

1. Conducting group participation on a shared writing piece will help strengthen students' writing.
2. As needed, think aloud about writing conventions.
3. Simplify the elements you required according to what students are ready for.
4. If students do not have the stamina for a multiparagraph essay, allow them to write a single paragraph piece.
5. Encourage students to orally rehearse their pieces with partners prior to writing.

Tools for Success

"Peace is a daily, a weekly, a monthly process, gradually changing opinions, slowly eroding old barriers, quietly building new structures."

—John F. Kennedy

Overview

This section includes practical and easy-to-use tools to support teachers when implementing the persuasive strategies and lessons provided in this book. Original texts are provided to support student learning and address the challenge many teachers have in finding age-appropriate and high-interest persuasive texts. There are also additional pieces intended for teacher modeling and reproducible student pages for practice.

Tools for Success *(cont.)*

Persuasive-Writing Vocabulary for Students

	DEFINITION	EXAMPLE
Audience	the people you are writing to	a political figure, a parent, the police department
Call-to-Action Statement	the part where you tell your audience to do something	Clean up the park now!
Claim	a statement of truth	Her claim is that cell phones in schools are a bad thing for students.
Closure	the end of your writing	Rephrase your purpose for writing the piece.
Credible	able to be believed, convincing	Anthony provides credible reasons for his opinion. That website is not a credible source because we do not know who published it.
Detail	something else you tell the reader to support your point	You need more details. Add a fact, an example, or more information here.
Evidence	facts that prove that what you claim is true	Do you have any evidence that bacon is unhealthy?
Fact	a true statement; should be true for everyone, not just you	Alligators are carnivores.
Genre	a type of writing	fairy tales, opinion writing, adventure
Illustration	a picture or a drawing	Please include a drawing or a photo of the museum for your reader.
Introduction	the beginning of your writing	We have a problem in our town that needs to be addressed: Lake Cosmo is polluted.
Issue	an important topic or problem	Pollution in Lake Cosmo is a big issue for our town.
Linking Words and Phrases	words and phrases that join your ideas	*because, and, also, another*
Logic	a way of thinking about something; reasoning	Supurna's mom failed to see the logic of letting her play before finishing her homework.
Opinion	a personal belief; may be true for some but not true for all people	Amusement parks are fun.

Tools for Success *(cont.)*

	DEFINITION	EXAMPLE
Persuasive writing	writing that tries to convince the reader to agree with the view of the author	a letter to a grandmother to persuade her to visit
Preference	when you like one thing better than another	I like cake better than cookies. Dogs are my favorite pet.
Purpose	the reason you do something	I wrote this letter to convince my principal that we need more books in the library.
Reason	a cause or explanation for an opinion	It is important for everyone to get exercise because exercise helps us stay healthy.
Reasoning	your thinking, reasons, and evidence to support your opinion	I know Langston thinks we should not have zoos, but what is his reasoning?
Sound Reasoning	reasoning that is clear, relevant, and makes sense	I think her reasoning is sound because she proved her points with facts.
Source	a book, a resource, a survey, a person, etc. from which you find information on a topic	I used three sources of information in my essay.
Stance	a person's point of view on an issue	Her stance is that students should choose their own seats in the cafeteria.
Summary of Reasoning	when you repeat your main point at the end of an essay	In this essay, I have proven that dogs make excellent pets because they are friendly, smart, and helpful.
Tone	the author's attitude or emotion in a piece of writing	Her tone in her piece about bear hunting was very angry.
Topic	the main subject of a piece in a few words or less	littering, animals, sports
View	the way a person sees things; stance	NieNie's view is that the zoo is the best field trip because she loves animals.
Voice	the personality of an author that is conveyed by his or her writing	I can really hear Jose's voice coming through in this piece. It sounds just like him.

Reproducible Items

Analyzing Opinion Writing

Type of Opinion Text ______________________________

____

Topic of Opinion Text ______________________________

____

Main Opinion on the Topic of the Text

____

____

Reasons to Support the Main Opinion

____

____

Evidence to Support the Main Opinion

____

____

Persuasion Score (1 to 10 with 10 being the most persuasive) and Why

____

____

Option 1 Soundness of Reasons and Evidence

What is the author's opinion?____

____

What reasons and evidence does the author give to support the opinion?

____

____

____

Does the reasoning make sense to you? Why, or why not?

____

____

Did the author change your mind or confirm your opinion? Why, or why not?

____

____

On a scale of 1 to 10 (with 10 being the MOST persuasive), how strong is this persuasive piece? Explain your answer.

____

____

____

Tools for Success *(cont.)*

Option 2 Soundness of Reasons and Evidence	Yes or No	Explain
Is the author fair to both sides?		
Does the author state reasons clearly?		
Does the author support each reason with convincing evidence?		
Does the author balance logic and emotion?		
Is the evidence connected to the reasons (relevance)?		
Are the sources credible?		
Did the author confirm or change your thinking? How?		
On a scale of 1 to 10 (with 10 being the MOST persuasive), how strong is this persuasive piece? Explain your answer.		

Tools for Success *(cont.)*

Soundness of Reasons and Evidence	Explain
What is the author's opinion?	*Students should go to school all year long. There should be no summer vacation.*
What reasons and evidence does the author give to support the opinion?	***Reason 1:*** *Studies have shown that students who take summer vacation lose a month or more of learning over the course of seven to eight weeks.* ***Evidence 1:*** *Harris Cooper, a specialist on year-round schooling, argues, "Students in year-round programs rate slightly higher in retaining learned material. The difference is even larger for students who are struggling in school."*
Does the reasoning make sense to you? Why, or why not?	*Yes, the reasoning makes sense to me. The author provides clear reasons to support her claim, and she uses relevant and credible evidence to support her reasons.*
Did the author change your mind or confirm your opinion? Why, or why not?	*The author changed my mind. I never thought I would want to go to school all year long. But she made me realize that it would actually be better to go to school all year because I would not have to relearn what I forgot, and I would still have as much vacation—just spread out differently.*
On a scale of 1 to 10 (with 10 being the MOST persuasive), how strong is this persuasive piece? Explain your answer.	*This scores a 10. She is very convincing. Before I read the article, I thought I would hate going to school in the summer, but she persuaded me that it would be much better to go to school all year long.*

Tools for Success *(cont.)*

Persuasive Writing COPS Editing Checklist	
Task	**Yes or No**
Did I check and correct my capitalization?	
Did I capitalize the first word of each sentence?	
Did I capitalize the names of people and places?	
Did I check and correct my order and usage of words?	
Did I use complete sentences?	
Do my sentences sound right?	
Did I use the word I meant (e.g., *two* not *too*)?	
Did I check and correct my punctuation?	
Did I use commas and quotation marks to mark direct quotations from a text?	
Did I end all of my sentences with either a period, an exclamation point, or a question mark?	
Did I check my spelling?	
Did I check the spelling of tricky words using a source such as the word wall, a dictionary, or an online reference guide?	

Aristotle's Many Ways to Persuade

Ethos Pathos Logos

Be credible

- be an expert
- be experienced
- be likable
- get your info from good sources
- be well educated
- use correct grammar and spelling

Stir emotions

- share your feelings
- describe your feelings
- use powerful visuals
- show emotion
- choose powerful words
- tell a story

Use facts and knowledge

- structure your writing clearly
- describe your experience
- add facts and statistics
- interview or poll others
- add expert quotes and opinions
- add examples and comparisons

Aristotle's Many Ways to Persuade

Ethos Pathos Logos

Be credible

- be an expert
- be experienced
- be likable
- get your info from good sources
- be well educated
- use correct grammar and spelling

Stir emotions

- share your feelings
- describe your feelings
- use powerful visuals
- show emotion
- choose powerful words
- tell a story

Use facts and knowledge

- structure your writing clearly
- describe your experience
- add facts and statistics
- interview or poll others
- add expert quotes and opinions
- add examples and comparisons

Tools for Success *(cont.)*

What I Think and Why
Main Opinion or Claim ____________________ ____________________
Reason 1 ____________________ ____________________
Evidence to Support Reason 1 ____________________ ____________________
Reason 2 ____________________ ____________________
Evidence to Support Reason 2 ____________________ ____________________
Reason 3 ____________________ ____________________
Evidence to Support Reason 3 ____________________ ____________________

Common Linking Words and Phrases

Also ______

What is more, ______

In addition, ______

Similarly, ______

Likewise, ______

In much the same way ______

However, ______

On the other hand, ______

Although, ______

First of all, ______

Second, ______

Third, ______

Furthermore, ______

Additionally, ______

Most of all, ______

Unfortunately, ______

In reality, ______

Not only will ______, but it will also ______

It says in the ______ that ______

An example can be found in ______

In ______ it clearly shows ______

For instance, ______

In this case, ______

Clearly, ______

As a result, ______

Therefore, ______

In summary, ______

All things considered, ______

I have argued that ______

Finally, ______

Persuasive Writing Planner

Main Opinion or Claim

____

____

Reason 1

____

____

Evidence to Support Reason 1

____

____

Reason 2

____

____

Evidence to Support Reason 2

____

____

Reason 3

____

____

Evidence to Support Reason 3

____

____

Call to Action

____

____

Topic Ideas to Broaden Writing Horizons

Myself

- allowance
- bedtime
- extracurricular activities
- food and flavors
- holidays
- movies, songs, video games
- personal heroes
- pets/family pet
- places to go/visit
- sports/sports teams

My Classroom and My School

- amount of recess time
- assemblies
- books, authors, characters
- cafeteria rules and menu
- class pets
- class trips
- classroom and school rules
- gum in school, homework, grades
- mandatory athletics
- noise in the library or hallway
- playground equipment school fundraisers
- school lunches
- school service projects
- school uniforms
- segments of the day/ subjects
- something you would like to change about your school
- treatment of students
- year-round school or vacation

My Community

- community events
- community gardens
- community service opportunities
- people who have made changes in your community
- local elections
- local laws
- public services (library, post office, etc.)
- public safety
- public transportation
- recreational resources
- something you would like to change about your community
- stores available in your local community
- traffic safety
- vandalism and litter

My Country

- cultural traditions (food, music, clothing, etc.)
- current events
- elections
- important landmarks
- laws
- people who have made changes in our country
- places to visit
- something you would like to change about your country

My World

- animals, animal habitats
- behaviors or practices that apply to everyone
- environmental issues
- important people or events from history and today
- inventions
- littering, pollution
- something you would like to change about your world
- space exploration
- technology
- wildlife, nature

Tools for Success *(cont.)*

Sample Cross-Disciplinary Project Plan

This plan illustrates how to connect content-area goals and concepts with persuasive writing.

<table>
<tr><th colspan="2">ENVIRONMENTAL STUDIES UNIT: PEOPLE AND THE ENVIRONMENT</th></tr>
<tr><th>Social Studies Focus Objectives</th><th>ELA Focus Objectives</th></tr>
<tr><td>Students will understand how people affect the environment.

The students will understand:

The environment may be affected by the actions of human beings in positive and negative ways.

Key Concepts:
◆ recycling
◆ water conservation
◆ wildlife conservation
◆ pollution
◆ overfishing/overhunting
◆ poaching</td><td>◆ Students will conduct research by reading informational text on environmental topics and choosing credible sources.
◆ Students will write opinion pieces in which they introduce the topics they are writing about, state opinions, supply reasons that support the opinions, use linking words (e.g., because, and, also) to connect opinion and reasons, and provide concluding statements or sections.

Key Concepts:
◆ to persuade
◆ topic
◆ issue
◆ fact
◆ opinion
◆ opening
◆ reasoning
◆ conclusion
◆ call to action
◆ audience
◆ visual support</td></tr>
<tr><th colspan="2">Cross-Disciplinary Multi-Genre Writing Project</th></tr>
<tr><td colspan="2">Students will choose one issue to practice researching, note-taking, and writing as a whole class. They will choose another issue to research as part of a small interest-based group.

Students will make claims and develop evidence-based reasoning related to an issue. They will compose and present their views in individual traditional essays, plus choose two additional genres to present their argument to the class (Example: persuasive poster and a PowerPoint presentation).</td></tr>
</table>

Sample Persuasive Reading and Writing Unit Plans

SAMPLE GRADE 3 UNIT PLAN

THE READER AND WRITER'S OPINION: A COLLABORATIVE AUTHOR STUDY
Grade Level: 3
Why Teach This?
In this unit, students will work in collaborative groups to conduct an author study and form opinions about the author's craft and his or her texts. Students will read several texts in a series, at their reading levels, to gain a deep understanding of the author and his or her series. Students will then write a book review on one of the texts in their series. We recommend breaking students into groups based on their reading levels and allowing them to choose a series that matches their purposes and levels.
Framing Questions
◆ How does studying an author and a series help us gain a deeper understanding of the story elements and the theme? ◆ When we read books, what things do we form opinions about? ◆ What type of series, themes, plots, or characters appeal to us as readers? Why? ◆ In what ways can sharing our opinions about authors help other readers? ◆ How can we share our opinions of authors?
Unit Goals
◆ Read closely to deepen comprehension and compare literary elements and the choices authors make across a book series. ◆ Develop speaking and listening skills and collaborative abilities by participating in small literature study groups. ◆ Cite specific text evidence to support their ideas and opinions about books within a series and the author of the series. ◆ Craft several pieces of writing connected to their opinions about their reading. ◆ Create and deliver an organized presentation on their collaborative group findings.

Tools for Success *(cont.)*

Anchor Texts and Resources
Various book series at your students' reading level, such as: ◆ A to Z Mystery series by Ron Roy ◆ Anna Wang series by Andrea Cheng ◆ Geronimo Stilton series by Geronimo Stilton ◆ The Lola Levine series by Monica Brown and Angela Dominguez ◆ Magic Treehouse series by Mary Pope Osborne ◆ Secret Coders series by Gene Luen Yang and Mike Holmes

Key Academic Words	Key Academic Phrases
◆ author's craft ◆ author's purpose ◆ chapter ◆ character ◆ descriptive language ◆ event ◆ dialogue ◆ key events ◆ persuade ◆ plot ◆ point of view ◆ problem/conflict ◆ series ◆ setting ◆ solution/resolution ◆ summary ◆ theme ◆ word choice	◆ The books (characters, events, settings, etc.) in this series are similar to ______. ◆ The books (characters, events, settings, etc.) in this series are different from ______. ◆ One theme that emerges in this book is ______. ◆ A theme that emerges across the series is ______. ◆ I think this because ______. ◆ My favorite thing about (author) is ______. ◆ My favorite thing about (series) is ______. ◆ My favorite book of the (series) is ______ because ______. ◆ For example, ______.

SECTION 6

Lesson Objectives in Reading and Writing

Lessons may be taught alternately (Reading 1, Writing 1, Reading 2, Writing 2).

More complex concepts may be explored for multiple days.

Many of these objectives are supported in the Strategy section in Section 4.

Readers learn the rules and behaviors for collaborative groups to help them run smoothly and be productive.

Readers use collaborative discussions to develop their ideas and opinions about books.

Readers gain a deep understanding of their reading by closely looking at the story elements (character, setting, key plot events, problem and solution).

Readers craft succinct summaries of their reading by focusing on the story elements.

Readers express opinions about story elements and cite text evidence to back their opinions.

Readers use textual clues to identify the theme(s) in their reading.

Readers compare and contrast the story elements across multiple books in a series.

Readers find out more about the author to make deeper connections to their books.

Readers express opinions about an author and use text evidence to back their ideas.

Readers make book recommendations.

Writers summarize for different purposes.

Writers examine and describe the structure and content of book reviews.

Writers notice how book reviews use strong and precise language to express opinions.

Writers respond to text elements in short written responses.

Writers plan the elements of a book review.

Writers capture the reader's attention by crafting strong introductions.

Writers use relevant text as evidence to strengthen their opinions.

Writers use linking words and phrases to connect their opinions and reasons.

Writers craft strong conclusions that leave the audience thinking.

Writers revise and edit their work with partners.

Writers prepare their book reviews for publication.

Writers present their book reviews to persuade an audience to read their books.

Tools for Success *(cont.)*

SAMPLE GRADE 4 UNIT PLAN

POETRY WARS: READING, INTERPRETING, AND DEBATING MEANING IN POETRY
Grade Level: 4
Why Teach This?
This unit emphasizes the close reading of poetry to consider and debate the meaning of poems. Students look closely at poetry, both at the word level and at the poem as a whole, to understand what meaning the poet may have intended and to establish their own interpretations of the poem's meaning, using text evidence to support their thinking. Through writing, students practice using the language of poetry and persuasion to explain their stance on the poet's intended meaning. They make plans to share and defend their views and compare their views to those of their classmates. The unit culminates with a poetry debate in which students craft arguments to persuade an audience that their interpretations are accurate.
Framing Questions
What clues can we use to interpret poetry? (In other words, how do we figure out what the poems mean?) What are the structures found in poetry? What techniques do poets use that I can use in my writing? What poetry mentors can I model my writing after? What language can I use to define and support my opinion? What is the purpose and structure of a debate? What is the best approach to persuade others to accept my ideas and interpretations of poetry?
Unit Goals
Read closely to determine the meaning of words and phrases and the significance of structural elements in poems. Read closely to examine details in poetry to form interpretations, citing textual and experiential evidence to support their thinking in order to persuade others of their view. Build speaking and listening skills through the oral presentation of poems. Compose original poems incorporating techniques to strengthen meaning. Write organized opinion pieces that defend their interpretations of poems. Orally present and defend their interpretations of poems.

Tools for Success *(cont.)*

Anchor Texts and Resources	
Selections from Ralph Fletcher's *A Writing Kind of Day*	Roald Dahl "Little Red Riding Hood and the Wolf"
Selections from Sharon Creech's *Love That Dog*	Pat Mora "Words Free as Confetti"
Arnold Adoff *Street Music*	Robert Frost "The Pasture"
Carl Sandburg "Fog"	S. C. Rigg "The Apple"
Emily Dickinson "In the Garden"	Valerie Worth "Dog"
Emma Lazarus "The New Colossus"	William Blake "The Echoing Green"
Ernest Lawrence Thayer "Casey at the Bat"	William Blake "The Tiger"
Grace Nichols "They Were My People"	William Carlos Williams "The Red Wheelbarrow"

Key Academic Words	Key Academic Phrases
alliteration	This poem reminds me of when (personal connection)_____.
assonance	This poem reminds me of (another poem, book, etc.) _____.
author's purpose	I think the poet's message is _____.
hyperbole	This poem makes me feel _____ because _____.
idiom	_____ is a metaphor for _____.
imagery	The big idea or theme of this poem is _____.
metaphor	This poem appeals to my senses by (give examples) _____.
mood	This poem paints a picture of _____.
onomatopoeia	I like how the poet _____.
personification	I noticed a technique this poet uses, which is _____.
poem	I have noticed something in many of this poet's poems: _____.
repetition	This poem is important to me because _____.
rhyme	My favorite part of the poem is _____ because ______.
simile	I agree with this interpretation because ______.
theme	I disagree with this interpretation because ______.
white space	

Tools for Success *(cont.)*

Lesson Objectives in Reading and Writing
Lessons may be taught alternately (Reading 1, Writing 1, Reading 2, Writing 2).
More complex concepts may be explored for multiple days.
Many of these objectives are supported in the Strategy section in Section 4.
Readers connect to poems for a variety of reasons.
Readers answer the question, *What is this poem saying to me?*
Readers notice how a poet structures a poem.
Readers interpret poems by focusing on feelings or the mood.
Readers interpret poems by focusing on strong images.
Readers interpret poems by focusing on what the speaker or characters do and say.
Readers interpret poems by considering the author's purpose.
Readers compare and contrast poems.
Readers orally read poems with a strong voice to convey the author's message.
Readers make recommendations of poems and poets to others.
Writers consider their opinion of poetry through a poetry inventory.
Writers look for poems that speak to them and that they can honor through tribute poetry writing.
Writers of poetry use strong word choices to create strong images.
Writers talk about what they notice in one another's poems.
Writers share interpretations of poetry in writing.
Writers add to their interpretations by providing reasons that are supported by evidence from the text.
Writers plan to defend their interpretations.
Writers debate using persuasive language and respectful disagreement to defend their thinking.
Writers reflect on their opinions of poetry by revisiting their poetry inventories.

SAMPLE GRADE 5 UNIT PLAN

MAKING THE CASE: READING AND WRITING EDITORIALS
Grade Level: 5
Why Teach This?
This unit focuses on providing opportunities for students to express their opinions clearly, present an organized and logical argument to support their claims, and write persuasively. In the reading lessons, the unit pushes students to closely analyze a series of mentor editorials to gain a better command of the genre. In addition, students conduct short research projects to gather information and evidence to support their points of view on a specific topic or issue.
Framing Questions
How can we use our writing to change the world? How can we use mentor texts to guide and inform our writing? How do you build a strong written argument? How and where can we find credible and relevant sources to support our ideas?
Unit Goals
◆ Read editorials closely to analyze the structure, features, content, and purpose of this genre. ◆ Research self-chosen topics, take notes, and organize ideas. ◆ Compare and contrast multiple accounts of the same topic. ◆ Examine and practice how to develop and present a strong argument to an audience. ◆ Compose and publish organized editorials that express and support their opinions.

Tools for Success *(cont.)*

Anchor Texts and Resources		
◆ your local, regional, or city newspaper ◆ Science News for Students (an online resource at www.sciencenewsforstudents.org) ◆ Time for Kids (both in print and online at www.timeforkids.com) ◆ Scholastic News (both in print and online) ◆ sample editorials included in Section 6		
Key Academic Words	**Key Academic Phrases**	
acknowledge argument conclude editor editorial evidence opinion opposition ordering periodical position stance support	**expressing your opinion** in my opinion based on the fact that I feel/think that because personally, I maintain that due to it is my belief that since **adding more** what's more in addition furthermore most of all not only will first of all	**acknowledging the opposition** some say that it is true that while it is true **showing** in this case it is obvious that clearly **concluding** all things considered I have argued that it is clear that

Lesson Objectives in Reading
◆ Lessons may be taught alternately (Reading 1, Writing 1, Reading 2, Writing 2). ◆ More complex concepts may be explored for multiple days. ◆ Many of these objectives are supported in the Strategy section in Section 4. ◆ Readers notice the structure and features of editorials. ◆ Readers can identify the purpose of an editorial as well as any supporting evidence. ◆ Readers choose a topic about which they are passionate and gather related research materials. ◆ Readers conduct research and take notes on a topic about which they are passionate. ◆ Readers round out their research by turning to and effectively navigating online resources. ◆ Readers compare and contrast multiple accounts of the same topic or event. ◆ Readers revisit mentor texts to analyze the craft of introducing an issue. ◆ Readers revisit mentor texts to analyze how writers build an argument. ◆ Readers revisit mentor texts to analyze how writers craft strong conclusions. ◆ Readers develop a bulletin board to collect interesting and relevant editorials over time.
Lesson Objectives in Writing
◆ Writers think about the issues that inspire them to make their voices heard. ◆ Writers analyze mentor texts and respond in writing. ◆ Writers consider their audience. ◆ Writers craft strong opinion statements about an issue. ◆ Writers plan how their argument will unfold. ◆ Writers choose visual images to integrate into and strengthen their writing. ◆ Writers craft powerful, engaging, and clear introductions. ◆ Writers draft organized and logical arguments to support their opinion. ◆ Writers craft strong, relevant conclusions. ◆ Writers publish and respond to editorials.

Tools for Success *(cont.)*

Checklist of Proficient Performance in Persuasive Writing

This checklist lays out performance criteria for written persuasive pieces (paragraphs, essays, articles, or speeches). These may be customized according to the developmental needs of your students and the requirements of your curriculum.

Task	Yes or No
Did I include an introduction?	
Does my introduction include: ◆ an attention-grabbing opener? ◆ a clearly stated opinion that states my point of view?	
Did I state an opinion on the topic?	
Did I provide at least one logical reason to support my opinion?	
Did I include evidence to support my reason?	
Did I include at least one of the persuasive-writing techniques: ethos, pathos, or logos?	
Did I include effective words and phrases to connect ideas?	
Did I maintain an appropriate tone?	
Did I include a visual or multimedia that strengthens the message?	
Did I cite my sources appropriately?	
Did I include a call to action?	
Did I include a conclusion?	
Does my conclusion include: ◆ a restatement of the opinion? ◆ a summary of the main reasoning?	

Persuasive Writing Editing Checklist

Students may use this type of checklist independently (with training) or in conference with a teacher.

When we edit our writing, we are preparing it for others to read. We check for errors in capitalization, punctuation, spelling, and grammar. Use this checklist to help you edit your own writing.

Remember to check for:	Yes or No
a → A **Capitalization**	
. ! ? **Ending punctuation**	
" " **Quotation marks**	
, Commas transitions pauses lists	
' **Apostrophes** possessives (Joey's dog) contractions (can't, won't)	
Complete sentences correct grammar different patterns no fragments no run-ons	
Paragraphs **PATS:** New paragraph for change of **P**lace, **A**ction, **T**ime, and **S**peaker Indent, skip line or use editing symbol	
Spelling	

Tools for Success *(cont.)*

Questions for Close Reading

Use these questions to spark discussion during read-alouds, shared reading, and small-group reading.

Questions for Close Reading

- What is the author's opinion or claim?
- What reasons did the author supply to support the opinion or claim?
- What techniques/words did the author use to persuade you?
- Are there any other points or techniques that may have helped the author's case?
- What reasons would you pose to counter the author's opinion or claim?
- Did the author successfully influence your opinion? Why, or why not?
- Do you know anything about the author's background that influenced his or her point of view?
- Did the author include visual images? How did the images impact the argument?
- How do you think the author prepared to write this?
- How does this argument relate to your life?

Persuasive Writing Samples

Additional persuasive pieces are provided for teacher modeling. Many of the samples are provided at two reading levels. These samples are noted by numbering them Version 1 and Version 2. Version 1 is a lower-level version, while Version 2 is for more advanced students. Student reproducibles that are used in the model lessons are denoted with a black outline. These can be reproduced for the classroom.

Opinion Pieces

Zoos: Good for Animals and People

Have you ever seen, in front of your very eyes, an animal with an eight-foot-long tail that eats for twenty hours a day and is strong enough to kill a lion? Well, if you've ever been to a zoo, chances are, you can answer yes to this question, so long as the zoo had a giraffe exhibit. If we didn't have zoos in the United States, most of us would never see such amazing animals, let alone see them up close and in a safe environment. The Association of Zoos and Aquariums (AZA), receives more than 175 million visitors annually, which is more visitors annually than NFL, NBA, NHL, and MLB attendance combined (http://www.aza.org/visitor-demographics/). Zoos are beneficial to people and animals in many ways.

Keeping Animals Happy and Healthy

It might sound surprising to hear that animals benefit from being kept in a zoo. In fact, zoos get a lot of criticism for keeping wild animals in captivity. A lot of people think living in cages makes animals unhappy and bored. Actually, the cages in a zoo are more like an animal's real habitat in the wild, with similar plants, trees, and food! The zookeepers also give the animals a lot of attention and take great care of their health, making sure they have toys to play with and get enough exercise.

Speaking of the animal's health, the zoo is actually a really great place for an animal to get sick. Zookeepers are highly educated animal doctors and scientists. If a lion has a cough or a cheetah hurts his leg, the zookeepers can nurture the animals back to health. In the wild, a sick animal might not survive and would be vulnerable to predators.

Protecting the Species

What's even better is that zoos are able to save animals from endangerment or extinction. Unfortunately, in the wild, there are people, called poachers, who hunt animals illegally because they can get a lot of money from selling animal products, such as furs and ivory tusks. If too many animals are killed, they might disappear from our planet forever. One success story is when zoos were able to save the California condors, a type of bird that almost went extinct. At one time, there were two dozen California condors, but the Los Angeles and San Diego zoos offered the birds shelter and safety. San Diego Zoo Global mentions on their website that "as of April 30, 2012, the population of California condors had grown to 405, including 226 condors living in the wild" (http://www.sandiegozooglobal.org/overview).

Tools for Success *(cont.)*

Educating Communities

Now, how do zoos benefit people and communities? Most importantly, zoos teach us how to care for the magnificent creatures that share our planet. Almost all zoos have educational programs to teach visitors about animal conservation. That means we learn how to take better care of the environment, and when the environment is healthy, animals are more likely to be healthy. This makes us better friends to animals, and we can feel proud of ourselves for being responsible.

Another benefit of having a zoo or opening a zoo in a city is tourism. The San Diego Zoo attracts five million visitors every year (sandiegozoo.org). Tourists spend money not just at the zoo but at local businesses that rely on a steady stream of customers to make a profit to stay in business.

As long as zoos treat their animals humanely, the animals will be safe, healthy, and happy in their specially designed habitat, and will bring more tourists into town.

Big Food, Big Soda: Ban Supersize Drinks

What if I told you there was something you could drink that tasted good? But if you bought it in a huge container and drank too much of it, your health would be seriously hurt. Don't you think most people would agree you shouldn't be able to buy it in a big container? Of course. But when that thing is soda, people insist that they should be able to buy as much as they want. This leads to diabetes and other serious medical conditions. The sale of supersize sodas should stop.

There can be no doubt that the sugar in soda leads to diabetes and other health problems. Americans have been gaining weight steadily for the past two decades. A large part of obesity can be traced to the sugar in sodas. "In addition to weight gain, higher consumption of SSBs is associated with development of metabolic syndrome and type 2 diabetes" (Malik et al. 2011).

Americans drink more soda than almost anybody else on Earth. "More than 15 billion gallons were sold in 2000. That works out to at least one 12-ounce can per day for every man, woman, and child" (Squires 2000). And the sugar in all that soda is making us sick. Stopping people from buying huge sodas won't prevent them from drinking soda—it will just help them keep the amount they drink to a reasonable level.

As for those who point to the United States Declaration of Independence and the part about "life, liberty, and the pursuit of happiness," you can still pursue happiness by buying a lot of regular-sized sodas.

Also, higher rates of diabetes and obesity not only make us much less healthy as a nation, they also make healthcare costs go up to treat these ailments, so we all end up paying the cost for supersize sodas.

So, ban the sale of giant sodas. It will help make us much healthier as a country. And maybe some people will even start thinking about drinking something better for them.

Texting Instead of Talking: Are Text Messages Destroying Communication?

"How r u 2day?" If that question makes sense to you, chances are you're an expert at sending text messages. Some people (mostly grown-ups) are alarmed by the amount of time young people spend on cell phones, and the spelling and grammar they use within their text messages. Even though not every text message is a masterpiece, they are an important tool for communication.

Like them or not, text messages are here to stay. In fact a recent Pew Internet & American Life Project study showed that teenagers send over 3,000 text messages per month! (Lenhart, Ling, Campbell, & Purcell, 2010). You may think texting is just a way to be silly with your friends, but they are actually teaching us to communicate our thoughts in a short, straight-to-the-point way. This is not easy to do! No one wants to read a whole paragraph when all they need to know is where their mom put their clean gym shorts! Sometimes it takes creativity—and yes, made up words—to write our messages in a short and simple way, but this is good exercise for our brains.

Of course if we are sending so many text messages, this means we are spending less time using our phones for their original purpose—making phone calls. However, text messages don't replace human interaction, and sometimes it isn't possible to make a phone call anyway. For example, if we are in a library it would be rude (and against the rules!) to make a loud phone call. A text message allows us to say a quick hello, or to let our mom know we made it across the street safely. Come to think of it, mothers should be glad that kids are so great at texting! It's also important to note that most of the time we use text messages to arrange a time to meet our friends in person: "Are you free tonight? Let's go see a movie!" See? Text messages bring us together.

Now, I suppose the point about poor grammar and spelling must be addressed. There is a special language used in text messages that would be unacceptable to use for a school assignment or to communicate with anyone other than our friends and family members. However, when we are communicating outside of school or work, we should be allowed to have fun with the English language! As long as we are responsible and make sure to use only proper English outside of text messages, there is no harm in having fun with friends on our cell phones.

Finally, let's go back to that surprising fact from earlier: teenagers send over 3,000 text messages each month. That is six text messages every hour. It is hard to believe that anyone would need to send that many messages in such a short amount of time. Sure, it gives a lot of time to practice the art of text messaging, but we should not let any one activity consume our lives or take up too much of our time. Text messaging is fine in small or medium amounts, and we can, and should cut back the amount of time we spend texting by asking ourselves, "Does this message contain important information that must be sent right now?" If the answer is no, put that phone down, do u hear me?

In conclusion, don't panic, text messages are not destroying our ability to communicate with each another. Texting make us creative, and able to say what we really need to say quickly and simply. Yes, it is amazing how quick and easy it is to check in with our friends, but we should not go crazy and send more messages than we really need to. This way we can be good company for the people that are right in front of us, and we can pay attention to our surroundings. Trust me, you'll be thankful when you don't walk into a street sign or trip over a crack in the sidewalk because your nose was stuck in a phone!

Buses Should Have Seat Belts

When the wheels on the bus go round and round, you'd better be sitting down. It is against the law to drive in a car without a seat belt. Why is it not against the law to ride in a bus without a seat belt, too? I believe that students who ride buses should also wear seat belts.

On the road, cars, trucks, school buses, and city buses all drive together at the same speed. But the people riding the bus are not wearing seat belts. Sometimes, they are not even sitting down. What happens if the bus has to suddenly stop or gets into an accident? With no seat belt to keep students in their seats, they could get very badly hurt.

Seat belts do not just protect the passengers on a bus—they also help the bus driver. The bus driver needs to focus carefully on driving. She has to pay attention to all of the other cars on the road. It is hard to think when people are moving around on the bus. If all of the passengers buckle up, the bus driver can concentrate on getting all of the passengers safely to wherever they need to go. Public school driver Stanley Serpente said, "I wish all my buses had seat belts to keep students calm, seated, and safe!"

Buses are like extra-large cars and should have to follow all of the same rules as cars. Next time you get on a school bus, buckle up. If there are not any seat belts, contact the board of education to ask why it is not mandatory to wear a seat belt on the bus. Make a case for seat belts now to help all students ride safely to school!

Head to the Hut by Melanie G

Ahhhhhh! You walk in and inhale the delicious scent of food coming from the kitchen. A kind waiter leads you to your small table by the window. The table is decorated with a fine white tablecloth and candles. Gazing outside, you see a brilliant bright-red bridge going across the deep, multi-colored water. Focusing on the water, you notice the light greens, blues, and purples of the silky surface. A pod of dolphins swims around playfully. Looking back inside, you observe the outstanding décor around the room, including a delightfully mounted swordfish and an enormous marlin. An ancient Indian drum sits by the bathroom doors. You laugh at the signs—Kingfish for men, Ladyfish for woman—that are nailed to the wooden doors. As you relax in your cozy chair, a waitress brings you a menu and asks what you want for a drink and places a basket of warm homemade bread on the table. You have arrived in Dolphin Bay, Florida, and are at the wondrous restaurant called The Seafood Hut.

The Seafood Hut is an outstanding restaurant that I would recommend to anybody who lives in or is visiting the area. I especially love the food there, particularly the scrumptious, delightful, award-winning New England clam chowder. I am addicted (and you would be too if you tried it!) to its creamy, silky broth and fresh, juicy clams. The potatoes are chopped to perfection, and the mixed vegetables are cooked just right. The soup could make any freezing penguin become as warm as a scorching scorpion. And trust me, that's warm! I also enjoy the yummy, juicy, cooked to perfection New York Strip Steak. If anyone from out of state is ever feeling homesick down in Florida, this steak is sure to cheer you up! It is so tender and thick that a starving whale would be full after one bite! Since I do not like fish, I asked my mother and father, who know a good restaurant when they eat at one, what they thought of the fish. They both said the fish was superb, and my mom said it tastes just as good as it did 25 years ago when she came to the Seafood Shack. Imagine that—amazing food for over 25 years!

I recommend The Seafood Hut for anybody who loves excellent food, attractive décor, and a spectacular view. If you enjoy perfection, come to this restaurant pronto to be amazed!

Speech for Class President

Hello everybody. Thank you for thinking of me for class president.

I think I would make a good class president because people like me. I am friends with everyone in the class. You can talk to me about your problems. I like helping people. I always try to help people. Yesterday, I held the door open for a lady with a stroller.

I also like solving problems. If I win, I promise you will be able to come to me if you have a problem. When other kids fight, I try to help stop the fight. I will always be a friend to everybody. I am also a very responsible person. I do my chores when my parents ask me to. I am on time for class. Sometimes, I stay after class to help our teacher clean up. I promise to do all the class president stuff as best as I can.

I want to make sure everybody has fun in school. I like it when we do fun stuff. If I win, I will try to get more recess time. I will get more field trips. I will make there be less homework. But I think we can also make the boring stuff fun, too. I will work with the teacher to find things to make class fun. I thought of going to the science museum for a class trip. Trips like that are fun, but we also learn. I am open to ideas for fun things to learn from. If you have an idea for something fun that we can learn from, you can come to me with your idea. I will try to get it to happen.

I am also a good leader. I usually get picked to be team captain at gym. I know how to help us win the game. I've won a lot of games as team captain. People want to listen to me because I will help us win. I do not yell at the other kids if they make a mistake.

I think I am the best one for class president. I will work hard for you. I will make sure you have the best time at school. School can be boring a lot of the time, but I promise I will make it as fun as possible. If you feel lonely, I can be your friend. If someone is mean to you, I will help you. Thank you for listening to me.

The Importance of Owning a Dog

The Humane Society estimates that between six and eight million pets enter animal shelters each year. Three to four million of those animals are euthanized. Another four million are adopted by loving families. In my opinion, adopting a dog is a no-brainer because there are too many dogs living in shelters that need homes and too many reasons why having a dog can make your life better.

Kids are constantly told to exercise instead of watch TV. Walking, running, and playing with a puppy are fun ways to exercise. Walks are also a perfect opportunity for grownups to get outside, too.

Another thing about dogs is that they make excellent listeners and secret keepers. Researchers have found evidence that having a pet in the house makes children better communicators and more self-confident. It also improves social skills like listening and understanding body language.

Sometimes kids lose things (our shoes), break things (by accident), or forget to clean up. Dogs do all of these things, too! By learning to care for a dog, kids are more responsible.

The last thing that must be mentioned is how much fun it is to be around a dog. This may not be as scientific as the other points, but it is not hard to believe that families with a dog must smile and laugh more often. Think about the silly things a dog may do: chase its tail, perform silly tricks, dress in silly rabbit ears on Halloween—and these are just a few examples.

Some people think it is a bad idea because of the money a dog requires. It is true that dogs cost money—you have to buy food and bring them to the vet. However, talking about how to save money, budgeting, and searching for deals makes for a wonderful learning opportunity.

Certainly, owning a dog is a big decision that must be carefully considered. However, the many positive benefits of a canine companion will surely be rewarding. Somewhere, a dog is wagging his tail, waiting for you to finish reading so he can lick your face and sleep on your lap.

Save the Tigers

Tigers are amazing animals. According to National Geographic magazine, tigers have been on Earth for around 2,000,000 years. Tigers are the largest of the cat family. They may be big, but they can run incredibly fast—up to 40 miles per hour! They are also very good swimmers.

It is tragic that there are not as many tigers as there used to be in the world. There are only about 3,200 tigers left. Just 25 years ago there were 100,000! The World Wildlife Foundation, a group that works to save endangered animals, says on its website that tigers are suffering mostly from three things: loss of habitat, competition for space with humans, and the effects of climate change. These are all things people can help control if they work together.

Everyone should help save the tigers by supporting organizations dedicated to tiger conservation. A world without tigers would be a sad, sad place to live!

Tools for Success *(cont.)*

One Topic, Two Views: Speeches

Sample Speech #1: Get Off the Gridiron!

Do you wear a seat belt while riding in a car? Do you hold a child's hand when crossing the street? Of course! Most people do. These things help keep people safe. So, why do we allow young people to play football when evidence clearly shows how dangerous it is?

Athletics are important for high school students. Participating in sports helps students become active and fit. Sports also teach important life skills, such as self-discipline and teamwork (Boot). However, the risks from participating in football are much greater than the benefits. Today, I will prove that football is too dangerous for kids and should be banned for students.

One reason to ban students from playing football is the danger of brain injuries called concussions. More than 60,000 concussions a year happen on high school football fields (Breslow). When compared with 12 other high school sports played by men and women, football had the most head injuries, with 11.2 concussions per 10,000 games and practices (Breslow). Athletes who have had one concussion have more risk of another one ("Sports Concussion"). The long-term effects of many concussions can be enormous. Students with concussions often have trouble with memory and concentration, making learning difficult. Recent studies of the brains of former NFL players who had head injuries show abnormalities (Dotinga). Athletes are more likely to suffer from Alzheimer's and Parkinson's disease, permanent brain damage, and other problems that include memory loss and depression (Daugherty). Head injuries also put players at risk of death.

Although it does not happen often, the leading cause of death from sports is head injuries. We should not expose young people to this danger ("Sports Injuries Statistics"). It is not worth playing a game that can destroy kids' health today and later in their lives.

Why target football when other sports are also dangerous? Clearly, football is more dangerous because violent contact is part of the game. In most other sports, injuries are usually accidental. In football, hard contact and tackling are expected (Strauss). Therefore, it makes sense that serious injuries are more likely in football than other sports. In fact, football ranks number one for catastrophic injuries, which are injuries to the spine, spinal cord, skull, or brain. It is interesting to note that cheerleading was in second place (Walker). How can we allow students to play a sport that is proven to be so dangerous?

To make matters worse, there is evidence that football may actually be more dangerous than statistics show. This is because some students are failing to report their injuries. In a 2012 survey of high school football players, "a majority indicated that it was 'OK' to play with a concussion and said that they would 'play through any injury to win a game,' despite being knowledgeable about the symptoms and dangers of concussions" (Graham et al. 2012). An NIH study suggests several reasons that students fail to report concussions. Because concussions can be hard to diagnose, some players might not know they have a concussion. Many athletes don't want to let the team down or lose their position on the field. Another reason is that players want to prove how "tough" they are. Some players might not know about the dangers of playing with a concussion ("Young Athletes' Concussions Often Unreported"). When athletes don't report concussions, statistics make football appear safer than it really is.

There are some people who argue that instead of eliminating high school football entirely, we should instead make it safer with better equipment. This is not yet possible. Recent studies have suggested

that while football helmets can prevent some serious injuries, such as skull fractures, they do not prevent concussions. Right now, no one knows how to make a helmet that protects from concussions (Shanman). Until there are helmets that can successfully protect players from the effects of concussions, we should not put young people at risk.

John Moffitt, a former NFL player, recently quit football after years of devastating injuries. He argues that the money and fame that come with being a successful football player are just not worth the risks (Belson). How many more players will have to suffer serious injuries before we stop and say enough is enough?

Recently, many states have begun to recognize the risks of football and have slowly introduced measures to try to make the sport safer for students. But it's not enough. Even former president Obama recently stated that he would think twice before letting his son play football (if he had a son). Before deciding to play football, think long and hard about the risks. Write letters to your school and town athletic departments demanding that they ban football or at least require that players use the safest equipment and feel safe reporting their injuries. Don't put our young people at risk! Get kids off the gridiron!

Sample Speech #2: Football Forever!

Statistics show that in 2012–2013, the most popular high school sport in America was football. More than 1,000,000 students participated on teams, almost twice the number of any other sport ("Most Popular High School Sports"). Even more amazing, recent data shows that 166,000,000 fans attended high school football games ("Attendance at High School Sporting Events Tops 500 Million")!

Recently, there has been debate over whether football is too dangerous for students to play. Yet all of these people support the game anyway. Are all of the players and fans being foolish? Should football be banned? No! While there are some dangers to students playing football, the benefits outweigh the risks. Football benefits the players and the fans in many ways.

According to U.S. News & World Report, students who play a sport have higher grades. They are less likely to drop out of school and more likely to go to college. They are also less likely to be obese. A study of top executives revealed that 95 percent of them played high school sports, where they learned useful career skills, such as leadership and teamwork (AOSSM). Football paves the way for many students to get into college to play. For a lucky few, there will be an opportunity for a high-paying career in the NFL.

Football motivates students to succeed in school, avoid illegal drugs and cigarettes, and develop a strong sense of self-discipline, confidence, and leadership (Boot; Koebler). Football also benefits the community. Ticket sales help schools raise money, and the community gets to enjoy the games and show school spirit. Clearly, there are many great reasons to play football, and I didn't even mention how much fun it is, too!

Lots of people think football is very dangerous, but it turns out that football has an unfair reputation when compared with other sports and activities. In fact, football is not much more dangerous than many other sports for young athletes. Bicycling, basketball, cheerleading, mountain climbing, ATV riding, and skiing are also sports in which athletes are injured frequently (Schoenberger).

Tools for Success *(cont.)*

According to a study by the University of North Carolina Center for Catastrophic Sport Injury Research, between 2002 and 2012, there were about three deaths per year because of football. The study showed there were more deaths from weight lifting, mountain climbing, and being struck by lightning than football! Hundreds die from bicycling and thousands from swimming, but no one is trying to ban those activities. In 2009, there were 35,000 deaths from automobile accidents, so driving to football practice is much more dangerous than being on the field (Boot).

Why is football a target when so many other activities are just as dangerous or more so? It obviously shouldn't be, unless people plan to ban these other common activities. Instead of banning football, it should be made safer. There are several ways to do this. An NPR report provides a list of suggestions for how to make football safer for high school players. High school football teams should adopt each of these suggestions, and safety should be made a top priority. One suggestion is to practice in a safer way. Most concussions in football are caused when players slam into each other. Texas has recently limited the amount of helmet-to-helmet contact permitted during practice. Other states should do this, too. Also, school football teams should limit the amount of time players are allowed to practice tackling drills. Referees and coaches should ensure that players are not tackling in dangerous ways. Next, high school football teams should make sure to have access to an athletic trainer with medical training. Trainers can treat and monitor injuries such as concussions to be sure they don't get worse. Another suggestion is to require high school players to take a medical test at the beginning of the season to be sure they are healthy enough to play. Finally, high school football players should be prevented from playing at any sign of a concussion until it is clear they have completely recovered (Calkins). Taking these measures would make the game safer for everyone on the field.

Football is one of the greatest sports in America. Players, coaches, and fans enjoy the combination of action, teamwork, and strategy every day. Some benefits of this incredible sport affect the entire community and may even last a lifetime. Sure, it's a little dangerous, but what true sport isn't? More safety rules would be a good thing, but eliminating a sport, the most popular sport, from our schools is not necessary. Let your schools, coaches, and communities know why football matters to all of us! Football is here to stay, and it should be!

Leveled Opinion Pieces for Differentiation: Personal Essays

Art Class Is a Necessity Version 1

President Barack Obama once said, "The future belongs to young people with an education and the imagination to create." When I was in school, arts classes were everyday subjects. These classes had grades just like math, science, and history. My art teachers would take attendance and then pull out their pianos or paints. They had their tools just like a science teacher has test tubes and scales. Some schools today do not have any art classes. I believe this is bad.

Studies suggest that students who have arts education do better in school than students who do not. Art helps kids think about subjects in different ways. When I started singing classes, I was given sheet music. On that sheet music were a variety of notes and rests, all with different numeric values. In order to sing this music, I was required to count, add, and subtract. In that moment, I did not realize how much I was practicing numbers because of how much I loved to sing. I was able to hone my math skills while simultaneously learning to sing music!

Certain people in schools feel music and art classes are a waste of time. They think students focused on art are not studying as hard for their other classes. When my friend Carmen and I started taking art, she found her love of painting. When we read stories in English class, she would paint a picture of the words we read. When she made these pictures, she would learn the words in the story better. So would the rest of the class. That was really wonderful.

Carmen did not stop reading because she started painting. I did not stop practicing math because I started to sing. Our art classes made us better artists while also making us better students and thinkers. I am glad that I was able to experience these classes while I was in school. I am confident when I stand up and speak in front of a crowd because of acting. I am able to listen better and add faster because of music and singing. I am willing to think outside the box and come up with new ideas because of painting.

Improving a child's imagination does not take away from their school experience. Allowing kids to explore as many subjects as possible helps them to forge their own path. Art is not an extra subject that can be tossed aside. Art is valuable and a necessity every child deserves to experience in school.

Art Class Is a Necessity Version 2

President Barack Obama once said, "The future belongs to young people with an education and the imagination to create." When I was attending school, arts classes were everyday subjects with grades just like math, science, and history. My art teachers would take attendance and then pull out their tambourines or paints, much like a science teacher would pull out her beakers. As I grew older, art education became less important. In fact, certain schools today do not have any art classes. This is unacceptable.

Research has been gathered that proves students who have art in their education perform better overall than students who do not. Art helps kids think about academic subjects in different ways. I was never great at math. When I began singing classes, I was given sheet music. On that sheet music were a variety of notes and rests, all with different numeric values. In order to sing this music, I was required to count, add, and subtract. In that moment, I did not realize how much I was practicing numbers because of how much I loved to sing. I was able to hone my math skills while simultaneously learning to sing music!

Certain individuals in the academic field feel music and art classes are a waste of time. They argue students focused on art are not studying as hard for their other classes. Based on my experience, this is false. My friend Carmen always struggled to read. When we began taking art, she found her love of painting. Then, as time went on, we would read a story in English class and she would paint a picture of the words that were described on the page. When she created these beautiful pictures, she would understand the text better, and so would the rest of the class. We suddenly had an illustrator to make the stories come to life. That was really exciting.

Carmen did not stop reading because she started painting. I did not stop practicing math because I started to sing. It was the opposite. Our artistic classes made us better artists while also making us better students and thinkers.

I am now an adult who works in an office. My main responsibilities at my job involve reading and writing. Sometimes, even in this office job, I need to put on a show or draw a picture. I am not the best artist in the world, but I am glad that I was able to experience these classes while I was in school. I am confident when I stand up and speak in front of a crowd because of acting class. I am able to listen better and add more efficiently because of music and singing. I am willing to think outside the box and express ideas in different ways because of painting.

Honing a child's imagination does not take away from an academic experience. Allowing kids to explore as many subjects as possible helps them to forge their own path. How can a student know whether she is the next Picasso if she is never allowed to hold a paintbrush? Art is not an extra subject that can be tossed aside. Art is valuable and a necessity every child deserves to experience in school.

Do Not Forget to Play Version 1

When I was a little girl, my mother told me I would grow up to be a woman in a powerful position. At the age of five, I had already decided I was going to focus on my future. I began wearing suits and carrying briefcases to school. Although I intimidated many of the students in my grade, the teachers and parents admired my passion and confidence. I read as many books as I could on being an adult. I focused all of my energy on my future dreams. When students were outside on the playground after school or during recess, I would stay inside, in my suit, and study. It was not until I grew older that I realized I had missed out on my chance to be a child.

Perhaps you have heard the old phrase, "You do not know what you have until it is gone." I did not realize how true this would be for many years. I spent countless hours hunched over my desk, practicing math problems and reading lessons. I became so wrapped up in perfection that in seventh grade, I cried when I got an 89 percent on a math test! My mother began to worry about how serious I was at being an adult. She asked me to go outside and play in the sunshine. She begged me to switch out my suits for jeans and T-shirts. She wanted me to smile. In my mind, she did not understand that I had a future to focus on. I did not have time to be a kid.

When I started attending high school, I decided to focus some of my energy on the arts. I began attending theater classes and performing on stage. I memorized monologues and wrote scenes. I thought, "Great! If I work really hard, I will be perfect at this subject too!" One of my acting teachers, Ms. B, gave me a C on my first performance. I did not understand. I had practiced and practiced. I knew every line of the scene. I did not make a single mistake. When I asked her why I had not gotten an A, she said, "Erica, this is a funny scene from a play, so play." I went home and immediately began working. I wrote out every single idea I had about my scene and made sure I knew everything perfectly. When I performed the scene again I got another C. Ms. B shook her head. "You are taking this too seriously, Erica. I need you to be willing to act like the kid that you are. Have fun."

As I went through my four years of high school theater class, I learned a very important lesson: theater is an art, and art cannot be perfect. No matter how many times you work on a scene or a line, mistakes will happen. Someone will forget a line or stumble over their words. There is no way to get the perfect grade. I decided on that day in Ms. B's class that I would take her advice and learn to play. At 14, I finally learned how to be a kid.

If you are driven to succeed, that is a wonderful thing. Studying hard and learning as much as you can are valuable and important. But do not forget to pick a bunch of flowers or go on adventures with your best friend. Read books for school but also for fun. Now at 25, I watch cartoons every day. I now wear T-shirts with superheroes on them and color in coloring books. I went to a great college and have a wonderful job. I am really successful and can still make time to be a kid. Do not be afraid to have fun. There is plenty of time in the future to be an adult.

Do Not Forget to Play Version 2

When I was a child, my mother always said I would grow up to be a woman in a powerful position. At the age of five, I had already begun focusing on my future. I began wearing suits and carrying briefcases to school. Although I intimidated many of the students in my grade, teachers and parents admired my ambition. I consumed as many books as I could on becoming an adult. I focused my energy on my future dreams. While other students wasted time outside on the playground after school or during recess, I remained inside in my suit, continuing to learn. It was not until I grew older that I understood I had nearly missed out on my chance to be a child.

Perhaps you have heard the old phrase, "You do not know what you have until it is gone." It is difficult to comprehend the gravity of this statement as a young person. I spent countless hours hunched over my desk, practicing math problems and reading lessons. Because I was wrapped up in perfection, an 89 percent on a math test resulted in tears! My mother, worried about how seriously I was taking life, asked me to wander outside and play in the sunshine. She asked me to switch out my suits for jeans and T-shirts and simply smile. In my mind, she did not understand that I had a future to focus on. I did not have time to be a kid.

When I began attending high school, my focus shifted from strict academics to the arts. I began attending theater classes and performing on stage. I memorized monologues and wrote scenes. I thought, "Great! If I work really hard, I will be perfect at this subject, too!" One of my acting teachers, Ms. B, gave me a C on my first performance. I did not understand. I had practiced and practiced. I knew every line of the scene. I did not make a single mistake. When I asked her why I

Tools for Success *(cont.)*

had not gotten an A, she said, "Erica, this is a funny scene from a play, so play." I went home and immediately began working. I studied furiously once again. I wrote out every single idea I had about my scene and made sure I knew everything perfectly. When I performed the scene once more, I got another C. Ms. B shook her head. "You're taking this too seriously, Erica. I need you to be willing to act like the child that you are. Have fun."

As I completed my four years of high school theater class, I learned a very important lesson: theater is art, and art cannot be perfect. No matter how many times I was willing to work on my scenes or monologues, I was never capable of preventing mistakes from occurring. Sometimes, I would forget a line or stumble over my words. Sometimes, another actor on the stage would make their own mistakes, too. There is no way to get the perfect grade. I decided on that day in Ms. B's class that I would take her advice and learn to play. At 14, I finally started to live as a kid.

A drive to succeed is commendable and respectable. Dedicating time to academics and consuming as much information as possible are valuable and important skills. But do not forget to pick a bunch of flowers or go on adventures with your best friend. Read books for school but also for fun. Looking back on your childhood as an older person is not always easy. If I could go back in time, I would ensure that I dedicated energy to enjoying simplicity as much as I enjoyed success.

Now at 25, I watch cartoons every day. I now wear T-shirts with superheroes on them and color in coloring books. I attended a prestigious college and have a wonderful job. I am really successful and can still make time for childish activities. Do not be afraid to have fun. There is plenty of time in the future to be an adult.

Leveled Opinion Pieces for Differentiation: One Topic, Two Views

Summer Vacation Is Important Version 1

Have you heard the news about schools getting rid of summer vacation? I really hope that does not happen! Summer vacation is important to kids for a lot of reasons.

Without summer vacation, we do not get to spend any time with our families. I want to be able to play with my little brother when I am not in school. After school, I have to do my homework. Then, I have to eat dinner and go to bed. If I do not have summer vacation, then I do not have any real time to play with my brother.

My teacher told me that if I am in school for the whole year, I will be a better reader and writer. I read a lot of books over the summer anyway. I do not need to be in school where I am forced to read and not allowed to play video games. This does not help me learn. It just makes me tired.

Have you ever thought about what it would be like to be in school for 12 months? I think that if kids were forced to be in school for that entire time, they would not like school anymore. Teachers like summer vacation too. Some of my teachers come back from summer vacation and tell me about all of the places they have visited. If we do not have summer vacation, they will not be able to visit anyone anywhere! That is awful!

I also think that the amount of time that we get off from school is already very short. If we are in school the whole year, we will not get any vacation time ever. We will always have to get up to learn and never have a chance to lay by the pool or enjoy being a kid.

My mother plans trips during summer vacation. Sometimes, we go for a walk or go to the park. If we are in school, she will have to go to the park by herself.

At the end of the day, year-round schooling is bad for kids. It will make us unhappy and not want to be in school at all. I need summer vacation to refresh my love of learning. I need the time off to sleep late and not be learning anything. If I do not have this, I do not think it will be good for me.

Summer Vacation Is Important Version 2

Have you heard the news about schools getting rid of summer vacation? I really hope that does not happen! Summer vacation is important to students for many reasons.

Without summer vacation, students are unable to spend time with their families. In order to get proper recreation and the chance to spend time with brothers and sisters, it is necessary for students to be out of school for an extended period of time. In my case, I do not get to spend extended periods of time with my little brother while I am in school. After school, I need to study and complete my homework. Then, my parents make me eat dinner, and pretty soon, I need to sleep for the next day. If I do not have summer vacation, then I do not end up with any significant time to play with my brother.

My teacher informed me that if I were to be in school for the entire year, I would become a better reader and writer. I personally read a lot of books over the summer already, and I already know that I am a fantastic reader and writer. I even have a blog. I do not need to be in school where I am forced to read every day and am not allowed to play video games. This does not help me learn. It just makes me feel tired.

Have you ever thought about what it would be like to be in school for 12 months? If kids were forced to be in school for the entire summer, they would not like school anymore. Teachers enjoy summer vacation as well. Some of my teachers return after summer vacation and tell us about all of the places they have visited. Sometimes, they have pictures to show us or a presentation that relates back to the subjects we are learning in the classroom. If we do not have summer vacation, they will not be able to visit anyone anywhere or come up with as many lesson plans! They would also no longer have pictures to show us at the beginning of the year. This is simply unacceptable.

I also think that the amount of vacation time we currently have during the summer is brief. If we are in school the entire year, we will no longer have any vacation time. Instead, we will always be getting up to learn. We will never have a chance to relax and lay by the pool or enjoy being a kid.

My mother also plans many trips during summer vacation. Sometimes, we go for a walk or travel to the park in a different part of my city. If we are in school, she will have to go to the park by herself. I also know that she likes reading to us, and she will not have as many chances to do this if we are always with our teachers.

At the end of the day, year-round schooling is bad for kids. It will make us unhappy and not want to attend school. I need summer vacation to refresh my love of learning. I need the time off to sleep late and not be learning anything. If I do not have this, I do not think it will be good for me.

Students in Year-Round Schooling Are Ahead Version 1

Year-round schooling is better for all schools. Year-round schooling is when students go to school all year with short, one or two week vacations throughout the year instead of having one long summer vacation. Year-round schooling helps students do well in school. All schools should introduce year-round schooling because it is better.

One reason is that students do not read and write as much on summer vacation. Studies show that because students are not reading and writing as much, they forget a lot of what they learned the previous year. In fact, they can lose about one whole month of learning. Harris Cooper, an expert, said, "Students in year-round programs rate slightly higher in retaining learned material. The difference is even larger for students who are struggling in school." By going to school all year, students keep learning!

Also, teachers have the same students for a whole year. This means that students and teachers really get to know each other and teachers have more time to help students learn.

Finally, when students are in school all year, their brains never stop growing. Learning is like exercise for the brain, and it is good to exercise every day.

Although some people say that students need one long vacation to rest their brains and do other activities, students would have the same amount of vacation time—just not all at once!

People also say that year-round schooling costs too much. It does cost more, but it is worth the money because it helps students.

Students deserve a chance to succeed at school, and year-round schooling is the best way to do that!

Students in Year-Round Schooling Are Ahead Version 2

All schools should adopt a year-round schooling model. This is when students go to school all year with short, one or two week vacations all year instead of one long summer vacation. Students in year-round schools perform better, especially struggling students. There are many reasons it is beneficial.

One reason is that students usually do not read and write as much when they are on summer vacation. Studies show that students lose up to a month of learning over summer vacation. This is called the "Summer Slide." Evidence shows that students who attend school year-round are more successful. Harris Cooper, an expert on year-round schooling, argued, "Students in year-round programs rate slightly higher in retaining learned material. The difference is even larger for students who are struggling in school." By going to school all year, students keep learning!

Also, in year-round schooling classrooms, students and teachers develop strong relationships, since they are in class together for an entire year. Teachers have more time to help students, and students have more time to learn.

Finally, when students are in school all year, their brains never stop growing. The brain is like other muscles in the body—the more we use it, the stronger it gets. When students stop learning for a whole summer, they can lose their stamina.

One counterargument is that students need one long vacation to rest their brains and do other activities. However, students would have the same amount of vacation time—just not all at once!

Students deserve a chance to succeed at school, and year-round schooling is the best way to do that!

Text Set: Personal Essay and Biography

Why Maya Angelou Inspires Me

Maya Angelou is my idol. Maya Angelou was an American author. She was also an advocate and a poet. During her career, Maya Angelou accomplished more than most people ever dream of doing. She published many novels, learned six languages, and traveled the world. She was raised in Arkansas in the 1930s, where discrimination was present. Discrimination made it difficult for Maya Angelou to gain access to education and opportunity just because of the color of her skin. She was also at a disadvantage because she was a girl.

The reason Maya Angelou inspires me is because the obstacles she faced at a young age did not stop her from following her dreams. Maya Angelou always loved art and poetry. She found a way to enroll in different art programs. She found a way to work full time and support her son as a single mother. She survived a really difficult early life.

Maya Angelou did not accept people telling her she could not do things. Instead, she became a successful African American female film director in Hollywood. She became a professor and earned 50 honorary doctorate degrees. She also worked for more than one United States president. How many people do you know who have accomplished so much in their life?

The other reason Maya Angelou is an inspiration is because she never stopped learning or trying to learn. She constantly tried harder and did better. She started her career in the arts as a performer, then she later became a director. She started her career in civil rights activism, then she went on to work for presidents. She kept writing her novels, too.

I believe that Maya Angelou is a good example of a superhero—not the kind of superhero that you read about in stories, but the kind of superhero who looked at the world and tried to fix what was wrong. She met people like Malcolm X and Dr. Martin Luther King Jr. She traveled all over the world. She read and wrote as much as she could in her 86 years of life.

As a writer, I have always wanted to say something to make a difference. Maya Angelou helped me realize I cannot just say one thing that matters. I have to constantly say things that matter and help people. It is the best way to truly make a difference and inspire others to do the same.

Maya Angelou Biography

Introduction

Maya Angelou was an American activist, writer, and poet. Maya Angelou's original name was Marguerite Johnson. She was born in St. Louis, Missouri, in 1928. Her parents divorced when she was three. She moved to Arkansas with her brother where her grandmother raised her.

Early Life

Her grandmother was named Annie Henderson. Annie was a very religious woman. She taught Maya Christian values. She was taught to treat people with compassion and respect.

Tools for Success *(cont.)*

In the 1940s, Maya moved to Oakland, California, with her mother and brother. She briefly attended school in San Francisco but left to become a cable car conductor. She returned to high school a bit later. At age 17, she gave birth to a son. As a single mother, Maya worked as a waitress and a cook.

Arts and Travel

Maya fell in love with the arts at a very young age. She longed to be an artist. She wanted to learn more and continue her education. Over time, Maya took dance and singing lessons. In 1954, she auditioned for and earned a role in the musical Porgy and Bess. While she was touring the world, she visited 22 countries and mastered six languages, including French and Arabic. She returned to the United States for a short time but decided to move to Egypt in 1961. During this time, Maya became an editor for the Arab Observer, a newspaper.

Activism and Service

In 1964, during her travels, Maya met Malcolm X, a very famous Muslim minister and civil rights activist. Maya was raised in Arkansas in the 1930s, a time when racism and segregation were still enforced in the American South. Her challenging experiences growing up were a reason she decided to return to the United States to support Malcolm X and others in the Civil Rights movement.

Accomplishments

Over the course of her career, Maya published more than 36 works and earned more than 50 honorary doctorate degrees from colleges around the world. She was a very driven woman who wanted to make a difference in the world. Her poetry focused on the African American experience in the United States. She spoke about race and opportunity. She spoke about being a woman. She wrote, produced, and directed multiple films. She was driven to make a difference. Maya dedicated many years of her life to activism. She was invited by multiple presidents to serve in different jobs over the course of her career. She worked for President Ford, President Carter, and President Clinton. She was honored with many awards, including the Presidential Medal of Freedom, given to her by President Barack Obama for the good things she did for others.

Maya Angelou passed away on May 28, 2014, at the age of 86. She had been working as a professor at Wake Forest University in North Carolina, still motivated to change the world for the better.

Book Reviews

Book Review: *The Knights of the Kitchen Table*

The Knights of the Kitchen Table, by Jon Sciezka, is about three boys. Their names are Joe, Fred, and Sam. The boys discover that a magic book given to them by Joe's uncle gives them the power to travel back in time. Poof! They travel back to the time of King Arthur. The rest of the story is about how they try to find the magic book so they can get back to their own time period. This is the first book in the Time Warp Trio series, and I think it is great because it is full of adventure and is very funny.

I loved how the book is full of adventure. For example, in the beginning, Joe, Fred, and Sam fight the Black Knight. The fight is very exciting and makes you wonder if they will win or lose. They win! They also meet other knights who take them to fight a smelly giant and an angry dragon. Sam tricks the giant by telling him the dragon said he was a weakling, so the giant and the dragon fight each other. The giant and dragon kill each other with a big explosion!

After that, people think the boys are heroes. They even do card tricks for Queen Guinevere and get knighted by King Arthur! Finally, Merlin the magician helps them get back to their own time.

The Knights of the Kitchen Table is also hilariously funny. One of my favorite lines is when the boys are about to get stabbed by the knight's lance. Joe says, "Three regular guys happened to find themselves facing death by shish-kebab." Another hysterical part is when the dragon makes fire at the same time the giant passes gas, and they both get blown up! In addition, it is really funny when the boys teach the stable boys baseball and the ball accidentally flies into Merlin's tower.

Every chapter of The Knights of the Kitchen Table makes you wonder what will happen next and keep reading. It can even teach you about a new time period in a fun way. If you like funny books with lots of adventure about time travel, this is definitely the book for you!

Book Review: *Judy Moody Gets Famous*

Have you ever had your picture in the paper? In Judy Moody Gets Famous, by Megan McDonald, we see just how far Judy will go to see her name in print. While Judy may be famous in her family for her many melodramatic moods and famous in her third-grade class for getting white cards, she has never had her picture in the local newspaper. Judy doesn't know what she's missing until her classmate, Jessica Finch, informs her that not only did she have her picture in the paper as champion of the regional spelling bee but she even won a tiara. Judy is jealous. Since she is not a very talented speller, she soon realizes that she won't be getting famous anytime soon for her spelling. She tries to think of other ways to become famous, and her failed attempts are always hilarious. In the end, Judy does not become famous, or at least not in the way she first imagined.

I enjoyed this book because it is really witty and Judy is a lovable character. The author, Megan McDonald, has a sharp sense of humor that makes this book very entertaining. For example, when Judy hears about her classmate's success at the spelling bee spelling the word artichoke, Judy thinks about how she can barely spell meatloaf. She "felt about as famous as a pencil." Determined to become famous, Judy tries out all sort of zany things. She carves GW on a chewed-up cherry pit and claims it belonged to the tree George Washington chopped down. She has her cat make toast in a talent competition for pets, but the closest she comes to fame is getting her elbow in the corner of a picture in the newspaper.

The ending of this book came as a surprise to me because Judy does not exactly become famous. Instead, she does something generous and thoughtful for someone else without getting any credit for it. She does a good deed but remains anonymous. This seems to be more satisfying to her than getting her picture in the paper for something small and silly, and it makes for a much more interesting story. This is a fun book with a helpful lesson at the end.

Book Review: *Bink & Gollie*

Bink & Gollie by Kate DiCamillo and Alison McGhee, illustrated by Tony Fucile, is one of the greatest stories about the adventures of best friends ever told. If you like Frog and Toad or the Ivy & Bean books, you have to read Bink & Gollie!

The book tells the story of Bink and Gollie through creative words and really fun pictures. Bink is very short with wild hair and a lot of energy. She is excited about everything from socks to goldfish, and she seems to always be moving or ready to leap into action at any minute. Gollie is very different from Bink. She is tall and a bit more serious. She talks very differently from most girls her age. The way she speaks can sometimes sound like a riddle or poetry. These two characters are what makes the book so wonderful. Even though they are very different, they are great friends. Bink can always understand what Gollie is saying even if she does not come right out and say it, and both girls love to roller-skate and go on adventures.

The next best thing about the book is the illustrations. The pictures tell their own story. Without looking at the words, you can understand each girl's personality. Bink has wild hair to match her energy. Even when she is standing still looking into a store selling colorful socks, you can see from the illustration that she is dying to go in and buy a pair. When Gollie sits on a couch, walks, or roller-skates, she seems very graceful and a little more grown-up than Bink. The other cool thing about the pictures is that they show you the girls' houses, and they look like every kid's dream. Gollie's house is in a tree! Bink lives in a small cottage just below the tree, and everything in her house is smaller than normal to match her size. The problem is that because the girls are different, they sometimes disagree. For example, Bink loves bright colors, but Gollie does not, saying, "The brightness of those socks pains me. I beg you not to purchase them." To stay friends, Bink and Gollie have to figure out how to do things they may not want to in order to be a good friend and bring happiness to each other and other people. You'll have to read the book to hear about their adventures and to find out whether they solve their differences and stay friends.

Book Review: *Dinosaurs Before Dark*

Dinosaurs Before Dark by Mary Pope Osborne is one of the most exciting books I have ever read! It is exciting because Annie and Jack find a magic tree house that is full of books. The story is crazy because they end up in a world with real-live dinosaurs! They meet three different dinosaurs and fly on one of them. It is a really exciting day.

I feel more like Jack than Annie because Jack is very serious. He really likes reading and wants to be a scientist. Annie walks right up to the dinosaurs without thinking. My sister is more like Annie.

I think the author wrote a really fun book. She makes me feel like I am in danger when the dinosaurs come. Jack and Annie run around a lot in the book, and it feels like a real adventure. I want to keep turning the page because I want to know what happens next. Her drawings of the tree house were also very helpful. I had trouble picturing the long ladder Annie and Jack climb. The picture helped me to see it better in my mind. I think this is a great book for any kid who likes dinosaurs or crazy stories! It was such a good book!

Book Review: *Supersize Animals*

You should read Supersize Animals by Melvin and Gilda Berger because it is filled with really huge animals! You can learn about dogs and turtles and rabbits all in one book.

I really like this book because the facts are next to pictures of the giant animals. It makes it easy to see what the facts mean about the animal. On the rabbit page, I can see how big the rabbit looks next to a regular-size rabbit. He is almost the length of a broom! On the dog page, I can see the length of his long legs. He is the size of a grown-up!

I also like this book because the animals in it are not animals I see every day. I went to the zoo the other day and saw gorillas and cheetahs. I did not get to see any of the animals in the book. I think that makes it better because I learned something new! If you want to learn more about supersize animals, then make sure to read this book!

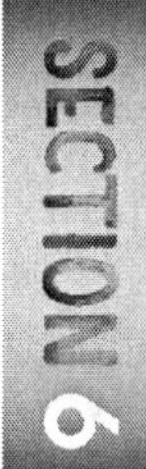

Tools for Success *(cont.)*

Infographics

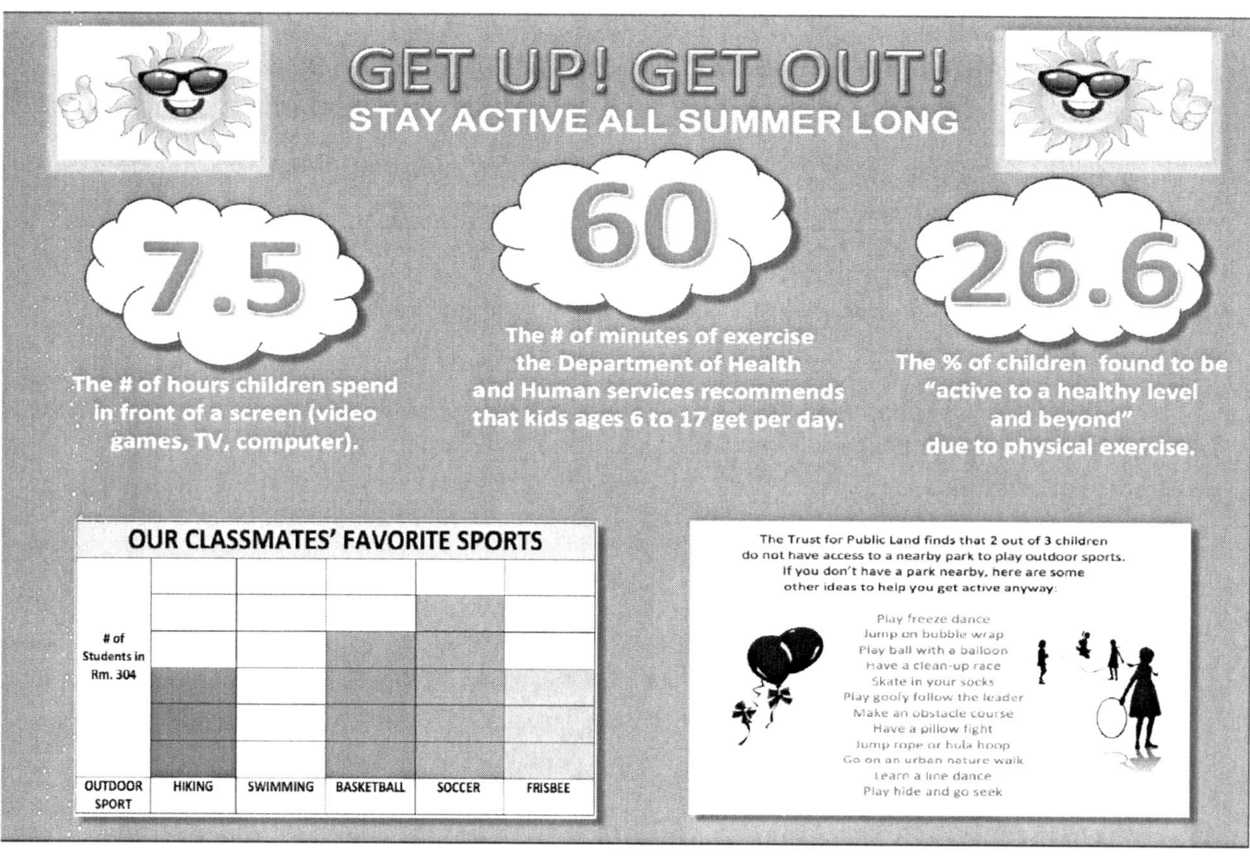

Why I Want a Giant Hamster Ball

A persuasive slideshow

by Abby, Gr. 4

Why do I want a giant hamster ball?

- Do you really have to ask that? It's the best toy ever!
- Why? It's a giant hamster ball! I can roll around in it, bring it to a lake or pool (it words in the water) or roll around on land. The fun never ends!
- It's complete safe, fun, and not even that expensive.

What is a giant hamster ball?

- It's a clear ball that humans can roll around in just like hamsters do. It's made out of soft plastic.
- Depending on the type, you either... A) get into the hole on the side of the ball and the hole stays open
- ...Or B) climb into the hole on the side and it has a cap over it.

What is the function?

- My friends and I can get great exercise while having fun! Everyone will want to play in it!
- Not only do giant hamster balls work on land, they are actually meant for water. In these pictures ahead, you will see many of them on water.
- Even though they are meant for water, they are also used on land. There are no specific "water-balls" and "land-balls."

Putting Our World
back together
1 piece at a time!

Advertisement

Standards and Correlations

Shell Education is committed to producing educational materials that are research and standards based. In this effort, we have correlated all of our products to the academic standards of all 50 states, the District of Columbia, the Department of Defense Dependents Schools, and all Canadian provinces.

How to Find

To print a detailed correlation report of this product for your state, visit our website at http://www.shelleducation.com and follow the on-screen directions. If you require assistance in printing correlation reports, please contact our Customer Service Department at 1-877-777-3450.

Purpose and Intent of Standards

The Every Student Succeeds Act (ESSA) mandates that all states adopt challenging academic standards that help students meet the goal of college and career readiness. While many states already adopted academic standards prior to ESSA, the act continues to hold states accountable for detailed and comprehensive standards.

Standards are designed to focus on instruction and guide adoption of curricula. Standards are statements that describe the criteria necessary for students to meet specific academic goals. They define the knowledge, skills, and content students should acquire at each level. Standards are also used to develop standardized tests to evaluate students' academic progress.

Teachers are required to demonstrate how their lessons meet state standards. State standards are used in the development of all of our products, so educators can be assured they meet the academic requirements of each state.

McREL Compendium

We use the Mid-Continent Research for Education and Learning (McREL) Compendium to create standards correlations. Each year, McREL analyzes state standards and revises the compendium. By following this procedure, McREL is able to produce a general compilation of national standards. Each lesson in this product is based on one or more McREL standards.

College-and-Career Readiness

Today's College-and-Career Readiness (CCR) standards offer guidelines for preparing K–12 students with the knowledge and skills in English and mathematics that are necessary to succeed in postsecondary job training and education. CCR standards include the Common Core State Standards (CCSS) as well as other state-adopted standards like the Texas Essential Knowledge and Skills (TEKS) and the Virginia Standards of Learning (SOL). The CCR standards listed support the objectives presented throughout the lessons.

TESOL and WIDA Standards

The activities in this book promote English language development for English language learners.

Standards and Correlations *(cont.)*

McREL
Uses the stylistic and rhetorical aspects of writing.
Uses grammatical and mechanical conventions in written compositions.
Gathers and uses information for research purposes.
College-and-Career Readiness Standards
CCRA.W.1 Write arguments to support claims in an analysis of substantive topics or texts using valid reasoning and relevant and sufficient evidence.
CCRA.W.2 Write informative/explanatory texts to examine and convey complex ideas and information clearly and accurately through the effective selection, organization, and analysis of content.
CCRA.W.4 Produce clear and coherent writing in which the development, organization, and style are appropriate to task, purpose, and audience.
CCRA.W.5 Develop and strengthen writing as needed by planning, revising, editing, rewriting, or trying a new approach.
CCRA.W.6 Use technology, including the Internet, to produce and publish writing and to interact and collaborate with others.
CCRA.W.7 Conduct short as well as more-sustained research projects based on focused questions, demonstrating understanding of the subject under investigation.
CCRA.W.9 Draw evidence from literary or informational texts to support analysis, reflection, and research.
CCRA.W.10 Write routinely over extended time frames (time for research, reflection, and revision) and shorter time frames (a single sitting or a day or two) for a range of tasks, purposes, and audiences.
TESOL
Standard 1 English language learners communicate for social, intercultural, and instructional purposes within the school setting.
Standard 2 English language learners communicate information, ideas, and concepts necessary for academic success in the area of language arts.
WIDA
Standard 1 English language learners communicate for social and instructional purposes within the school setting.
Standard 2 English language learners communicate information, ideas, and concepts necessary for academic success in the content area of Language Arts.

References Cited

Andriessen, Jerry. 2006. "Arguing to Learn." In *Handbook of the Learning Sciences*, edited by R. Keith Sawyer, 443–61. New York: Cambridge University Press.

Biancarosa, Gina, and Catherine Snow. 2006. *Reading Next—A Vision for Action and Research in Middle and High School Literacy: A Report to Carnegie Corporation of New York*, 2nd ed. Washington, DC: Alliance for Excellent Education.

Carnegie Council on Advancing Adolescent Literacy. 2010. *Time To Act: An Agenda for Advancing Adolescent Literacy for College and Career Success*. New York, NY: Carnegie Corporation of New York.

Crowhurst, Marion. 1990. "Teaching and Learning the Writing of Persuasive/Argumentative Discourse." *Canadian Journal of Education / Revue Canadienne De L'éducation* 15, no. 4 (Autumn): 348–59. https://doi.org/10.2307/1495109.

Freedman, Aviva. 1996. "Genres of Argument and Arguments as Genres." In *Perspectives on Written Argument*, edited by Berrill, Deborah P. Cresskill, NJ: Hampton Press.

Gerber, Hannah R., and Debra P. Price. 2011. "Twenty-First-Century Adolescents, Writing, and New Media: Meeting the Challenge with Game Controllers and Laptops." *The English Journal* 101, no. 2: 68–73.

Graff, Gerald, and Cathy Birkenstein. 2010. *They Say, I Say: The Moves That Matter in Academic Writing*. New York: W.W. Norton & Company.

Graham, Steve, Alisha Bollinger, Carol Booth Olsen, Catherine D'Aoust, Charles MacArthur, Deborah McCutchen, and Natalie Olinghouse. 2012. *Teaching Elementary School Students to Be Effective Writers*. Washington, DC: National Center for Education Evaluation and Regional Assistance, Institute of Education Sciences, U.S. Department of Education. https://ies.ed.gov/ncee/wwc/PracticeGuide/17.

Hillocks, George, Jr. 2010. "Teaching Argument for Critical Thinking and Writing: An Introduction." *The English Journal*, 99, no. 6 (July): 24-32.

Johnson, David W., and Roger T. Johnson. 2009. "Energizing Learning: The Instructional Power of Conflict." *Educational Researcher*, 38, no. 1 (January): 37–51.

Lange, Maggie. 2014. "59 Percent of Tiny Children Use Social Media." The Cut. https://www.thecut.com/2014/02/over-half-kids-social-media-before-age-ten.html.

National Governors Association Center for Best Practies, Council of Chief State School Officers. 2010. "Common Core State Standards." Washington, DC: National Governors Association Center for Best Practices, Council of Chief State School Officers.

NCTE (National Council of Teachers of English). 2016. "NCTE Beliefs about the Teaching of Writing, 2016." NCTE Comprehensive News. http://www.ncte.org/positions/statements/writingbeliefs.20%.

Newell, George E., Richard Beach, Jamie Smith, Jennifer VanDerHeide, Deanna Kuhn, and Jerry Andriessen. 2011. "Teaching and Learning Argumentative Reading: A Review of Research." *Reading Research Quarterly* 46, no. 3 (July/August/September): 273–304.

References Cited *(cont.)*

Reznitskaya, Alina, Richard C. Anderson, and Li-Jen Kuo. 2007. "Teaching and Learning Argumentation." *The Elementary School Journal,* 107(5): 449–72.

Stahl, Steven A. 2005. "Four Problems with Teaching Word Meanings (And What to Do to Make Vocabulary an Integral Part of Instruction)." In *Teaching and Learning Vocabulary: Bringing Research to Practice,* edited by Elfrieda H. Hiebert and Michael L. Kamil, 95–114. Mahwah, NJ: Lawrence Erlbaum.

Notes